D0482181

Living a Year of Kaddish

ALSO BY ARI L. GOLDMAN

The Search for God at Harvard
Being Jewish:
The Spiritual and Cultural Practice of Judaism Today

Living
a Year
of Kaddish

Ari L. Goldman

Schocken Books, New York

Portions of this book previously appeared in Chai Magazine
and Moment Magazine.

Library of Congress Cataloging-in-Publication Data
Goldman, Ari L., 1949–
    Living a year of Kaddish / Ari L. Goldman.
        p.   cm.
    ISBN 0-8052-4184-1
    1. Goldman, Ari L., 1949—Religion.   2. Jewish mourning
customs.
    3. Bereavement—Religious aspects—Judaism.   4. Consolation
(Judaism)   I. Title.

    E184.37.G65 A3 2003
    296.4'45'092—dc21
    [B]   2002042498

www.schocken.com
Book design by Iris Weinstein
Printed in the United States of America
First Edition

2   4   6   8   9   7   5   3   1

TO MY CHILDREN,

Adam, Emma, and Judah

After the grave is covered by earth, the son takes off his shoes, walks a few steps from the cemetery and says kaddish, for it is a prayer that renews the world.

—RABBI JOSEPH CARO, *in his sixteenth-century code of Jewish law, the* Shulchan Aruch

Contents

Living a Year of Kaddish

Prologue

I turned fifty in the waning days of the last century. The very next day, on Thursday, September 23, 1999, my father, Marvin Goldman, died of a heart attack at his home in Jerusalem, at the age of seventy-seven. His death was a harsh introduction to my much anticipated fifties.

I had decided to enter my sixth decade with a party for my closest friends at my Manhattan synagogue. I love a party, especially when I am the guest of honor. We drank Champagne, snacked on pastries and strawberries, and a few of us danced late into the night. My wife, Shira, and I let our kids stay up long, long past their bedtime—and ours—even though there was school and work the next day. I had insisted that the party be precisely on my birthday, September 22, and not on the weekend before or after. I knew that, given our helter-skelter lives, we'd never be able to arrange a party *prior* to my birthday and, if we were to delay even a day, months would pass before we'd actually get around to it. In retrospect, I made the right decision, although, as it turned out, for a completely unanticipated reason.

The morning after my party, we woke up all groggy and in a happy panic. We had ten minutes to get the kids ready for the school bus and just a few minutes more to get ourselves to work. Later that day, the call came. My father, who had lived in Israel since his retirement seven years earlier, collapsed after a quiet walk through the Jerusalem neighborhood he loved. By nightfall, he was dead. Jewish law requires that the funeral be held as soon as possible after death, and because the next day was Shabbat, on which funerals cannot take place, there was no way I could make it to the funeral. My father was buried early Friday morning in the plot he and his second wife purchased on Har HaMenuchot, the Hill of Eternal Rest, on the out-skirts of Jerusalem.

I had lost my mother four years earlier, so I knew the Jewish customs of mourning firsthand. I donned a white shirt and made a rip in the left side, baring my breast in grief. I sat close to the floor, on a low chair, in my living room, in my stockinged feet. Friends and relatives came to visit. "May the Holy One console you together with those who mourn for Zion and Jerusalem," they said, using the ancient Hebrew formula for comforting mourners. But for me, the traditional week-long period of mourning, called *shiva* (after the Hebrew word for seven), lasted only one day. My rabbi explained that *shiva* is canceled out by the onset of a festival. On Friday night, the Jewish festival of Sukkot began, a holiday that, as it happens, is known as "the season of our joy."

My eleven-year-old daughter, Emma, was the first one

to plant the idea. "Do you think Grandma and Grandpa are married again in heaven?" she asked, with the innocence that only a pre-teen can muster. "What? Married again?" I was somewhat taken aback. My parents had been divorced forty-four years earlier, when I was six. I could hardly imagine them married on this earth; how could they possibly be married in heaven? In the wake of the divorce, all signs that they had been together were obliterated. Their wedding album was incinerated, and all early family photographs destroyed. I had no memory of even seeing a picture of my parents together.

Still, I felt strangely liberated and comforted by the image Emma suggested. I realized that, with both my parents gone, I was, for the first time in forty-four years, no longer the child of divorce. Being the child of divorce had significantly shaped the person I had become, profoundly influencing virtually everything in my life, from my faith to my choice of profession. I clung tenaciously to Orthodox Judaism, the faith of both my parents, as one would cling to an ancestral home, because, with divorce, there is no ancestral home. Orthodox practice was the place I could always go back to. I became a journalist in large part because I had been taught, from the age of six, to entertain two widely divergent approaches to life, my mother's and my father's. One was flamboyant, the other modest. One was often miserly, the other gave it all away. One was punctual, the other didn't know what being on time meant. One read novels, the other studied sacred texts. One always sat in the front row, the other hid in the back. If I could handle my parents, the conflicts between Republicans and Democrats, Arabs and Israelis, Catholics and Protestants, Hindus and Christians, labor and management, rich and poor would be easy to negotiate.

At the age of fifty, I was no longer the child of divorce. I was no longer the child of anyone. Losing my parents altered my view of myself—and of them—in ways I had not anticipated. My year of mourning, for all its hardships, became a time of insight and growth.

It was a painful year, but one that I want to hold on to and, through this book, share with others. Losing a parent is a rite of passage for which no one is prepared. There is no such thing as a good death. My parents were very different in life and just as different in the ways that they died: my father in an instant, far away, and my mother of cancer, slowly and painfully, as we stood by, able to do little but lessen the pain. They died at opposite ends of the year, my mother in April and my father in September. And they were buried on different continents, my mother in New York and my father in Jerusalem. But in the year after my father's death, I often mourned for them as one. Despite all their differences, both of my parents believed in the discipline and power of prayer. My mother was active in her Orthodox synagogue and went most Saturdays, in particular on the Saturdays when the blessing of the new moon was recited, which marked the approach of a new month on the Hebrew calendar. My father's life revolved around the synagogue, especially in his later years. He attended services every morning, and often went to the afternoon service as well. In the year after his death, I went to *shul* every morning, too, ostensibly to say *kaddish*, the Jewish prayer recited to honor the dead, but on a deeper level to stand in for him and for my mother. They prayed; now I pray.

Mourning also became a time for mentoring and modeling. I lost my father, I reasoned, but I myself am still a father. In the year of mourning for my dad, Emma turned twelve, Adam turned sixteen, and our youngest, Judah, turned five. More than ever before, I insisted that they accompany me on Saturday to the synagogue where we pray. I needed them to see me saying *kaddish* for their grandfather. As my friend Rabbi Michael Paley told me when he was saying *kaddish* for his sister, the act of saying *kaddish* in the presence of your kids is like sitting them down and saying, "Hey, look what I'm doing. Take notes. You'll do this for me someday." For me, *kaddish* was as much of a chain as it was a prayer. It was a chain that in some way continued to connect me to my parents, and will some day connect me to my children.

And, finally, mourning became a time of community. As is the custom, in the year following my father's death I attended synagogue not only on Saturdays with the kids, but the other six days of the week as well, because according to Jewish law *kaddish* can be recited only in the presence of a *minyan*, the quorum of ten required for Jewish communal prayer. I was a regular on Saturdays at Ramath Orah, an Orthodox synagogue near my Manhattan home, which I'd joined shortly after we moved to the neighborhood seven years earlier. But going daily, I discovered, was different. The worshipers who answered "amen" to my *kaddish* every morning for a year eventually became my extended family. Some were fellow *kaddish*-sayers, others simply felt strongly about saying the morning prayers as part of a *minyan*, and still others had their own complex reasons for showing up every morning at Ramath Orah at 7:00 A.M. Among them was Philip, a Polish Holocaust survivor; Allan, a *New York Times* music critic; Lou, a venerable Columbia law professor; James, an eccentric statistician; and Chris, a young man in the process of conversion to Judaism. There was even the occasional woman worshiper although, as Ramath Orah is an Orthodox *shul*, women cannot be counted as part of the *minyan*. We came for prayer and we prayed, but we also talked, joked, laughed, and gossiped. We shared each other's stories and helped dissolve each other's pain. We became a community in the very best sense of the word; we knew that as individuals we were bound to the earth, but as a *minyan* we could reach the very gates of heaven. My *kaddish* connected me to my family, but it was empowered by my community. The story of my year of *kaddish* starts with me, but it derives meaning and context through the people I touched and the people who touched me every morning.

Fall

1

The last time I saw my father was in August 1999, one month before he died. I was in Israel on university business, mapping out a trip to the Holy Land as part of a spring seminar that I teach at Columbia University's Graduate School of Journalism. At that point, I hadn't seen my dad in a year and I could tell immediately that his health had deteriorated.

My father was a vigorous man who, curiously, became more relaxed and more adventurous with age, especially after he moved to Jerusalem in 1992. Six days a week he went to a *daf yomi* class in the Orthodox neighborhood of Geulah, a short drive from his home. *Daf yomi* is a system of study in which a folio page of Talmud is studied each day; at that rate, the entire Talmud (all 2,711 pages) is covered in a little over seven years. For my dad, *daf yomi* was part intellectual, part devotional (the study of Talmud is in itself meritorious), and part social event. His *daf yomi* study group was made up of about thirty men in their seventies, eighties, and even nineties, most of them from the United States, but some also from England, South Africa, and Australia. English was the language of discourse, although the text was read in the Talmud's original Hebrew and Aramaic.

The class was led by Rabbi Eliezer Simonson, who like many of his aging *daf yomi* students was a retired American pulpit rabbi. My father had spent his life buying, selling, and managing real estate in Hartford, Connecticut, and retired to Israel at the age of seventy. But he too was a rabbi, privately ordained in 1944 after graduating from Yeshiva University in New York. Several of the other men in his Jerusalem *daf yomi* class were, in fact, classmates of his at Yeshiva University. Here, some fifty years later, after raising families and building careers, they were together again, reading the very same texts they had studied as young men. Shira, our kids, and I spent the academic year of 1997–1998 in Jerusalem, and during that time, I sometimes joined Dad at *daf yomi.* He introduced me to his friends with great enthusiasm, and then we sat down to study. I was surprised by how easily I fit into his world of Torah learning, a world I had drifted away from.

In the year since I'd last seen him, Dad's doctors had discovered cancer in his right lung. They had taken out the lower lobe and were confident that they'd gotten all of the cancer, but the operation seriously weakened his heart. He recovered enough to resume his cherished *daf yomi* routine, but he could no longer drive to the class in his own car. Either friends would pick him up or he'd take the Number 14 bus right on his corner. He walked slowly and with a cane. But his spirits were good. He was excited that

I was visiting and he encouraged me to stay in the extra room in his apartment on Lloyd George Street. But I was traveling on an expense account, I told him, and I was looking forward to staying at the new Jerusalem Hilton. I promised to take my Shabbat meals with him.

I arrived in Israel on a Friday morning, took care of some business, tried to catch up on my jet lag (I can never sleep on the plane), and then met Dad at his apartment for the walk to synagogue. It was a walk that we'd taken together many times before—down the main thorough-fare of Emek Refaim, across the railroad tracks over which trains never ran on Shabbat to the neighboring commu-nity of Bakka, and then down Yair Street to the old domed-roof Yael Synagogue.

My father's gait was unsteady, and he leaned heavily on my arm. What was normally for him a fifteen-minute walk, was taking twice as long. He stopped often, ostensi-bly to point out a new store along Emek Refaim or to lis-ten to my answer to a question he asked me about my children. I remember feeling frustrated at how slowly he was walking and how often he stopped, especially on the way home from *shul.* He never complained about feeling sick, so I thought he was just dawdling. But by the time we returned to his apartment and he assumed his place at the head of the table, it was like old times. He sang *Shalom Aleichem,* the opening song of the Friday-night Sabbath meal, made *kiddush* over the wine, made *hamotzei* over the *challah,* and sang his traditional family Sabbath songs. His wife, Teme, served a home-cooked dinner of gefilte fish, salad, chicken soup, and chicken. Dad ate with obvious pleasure, brought me up to date on our many Israeli relatives, and asked me for more news of my children and of Shalom and Dov, my two brothers, who also live in America and made regular visits to see him in Israel.

I told my father about the project that had brought me to Israel, and how I planned to return with my class in March 2000 for the expected visit of Pope John Paul II to the Holy Land. We spoke about the possibility of my bringing my family along, either before or after the class trip. Dad said that if we all came, he'd make a special bat mitzvah party for Emma, just like the bar mitzvah party he'd made for Adam in 1997, during the year we had spent in Israel while I was teaching at the Hebrew University of Jerusalem. "I may not believe in equal rights," he joked, "but I believe in equal opportunity. Emma should have a party too."

Sitting in my father's apartment, I found it easy to forget how frail he had looked during our walk to and from the synagogue. I focused instead on how vigorous he seemed at the table. We spoke eagerly about the future.

I went about my business during the next few days, planning the upcoming trip. I met with tour operators and with religious and government officials, and I journeyed to the north of Israel to visit some of the *kibbutzim* where I was thinking of housing my students during our trip. I checked in with Dad by phone each day. He was very interested in the places I was visiting and in how I was getting around by train and bus. I told him I'd be back on Wednesday and had an 8:00 A.M. flight to New York the next morning. "Don't check back into the Hilton," he pleaded. "You'll have to get up at 4:00 in the morning and leave for the airport at 5:00. It's not worth it." I reminded him that I wasn't paying for it myself. "C'mon," he said, "stay with me. I've got the room."

It means a lot to him to have me under his roof, I realized. As a father myself, I know how good it feels to go around to all the bedrooms of my home late at night and see my children sleeping, safe and sound. When I'm home, it's my nightly ritual. Why should I deny my dad that pleasure? God knows, he didn't have that feeling often as a young father. I imagined him in Hartford, going around to the rooms where my brothers and I used to sleep and seeing only empty beds. After my mother left him in 1956, the three of us lived with her in New York and saw my father only on occasional weekends and Jewish holidays. How hard it must have been on him. "Sure," I said. "Why check into a hotel? I'm staying with you."

When I got to his apartment, we talked more about my sojourn up north. My father, who was just discovering public transportation after a lifelong love affair with cars, questioned me about routes and schedules and timetables. I told him about the great views of the Mediterranean on the train trip from Tel Aviv to Haifa, about how modern the trains are (they even have outlets for laptops), and about the seedy Tel Aviv bus station, where I picked up a bus to Jerusalem. He seemed to delight in my ability to get around without a car (I happen to hate driving). "I'm very proud of the way you did that," he said. The words struck me. I stared at him, sitting in his V-neck T-shirt and pajama bottoms, with a cup of iced coffee in front of him. In a sense I'd been waiting to hear that my whole life. "I'm very proud of you."

My dad did not support me in my career choice; he wanted me to be a doctor. He was certain that journalism would be the death of my Orthodoxy. "How can you be a Sabbath observer and a journalist?" he asked. "Impossible," he answered. I've spent my life trying to prove him wrong. I believed—and continue to believe—that I can at the same time be true to my faith and excel at my profession. Sure, I've made some compromises along the way, but even after all these years and all those compromises, my essential Orthodoxy remains intact. In my twenty-five-year career, I've written more than 1,000 articles for the *New York Times*. I wrote a book (which I know he didn't like for a myriad of reasons, including its portrayal of my parents' divorce), and I became a professor at Columbia. None of it seemed to please him. Why now, after mastering Israeli public transportation, was I a source of pride? Was he talking about my ability to navigate the Israel he loved, or was he taking the whole measure of my life and finding me suddenly worthy? I wasn't quite sure, but I do remember that I went to sleep quite happy that night.

My father wasn't much of a sleeper. Insomniac might be a better word. Soon after I got up at 4:00 A.M. to catch my plane, I heard him in the living room. He was opening and closing the glass doors of the wooden breakfront. He wished me a particularly enthusiastic "good morning" and mischievously handed me a silver *kiddush* cup and a silver *bessomim* box, the spice holder used during *havdala,* the prayer said at the conclusion of Shabbat. "These are for you," he said. "I want you to have them." My first reaction was: I wonder if he asked Teme. She was particularly proud of their silver collection and here he was giving part of it away. But she was fast asleep in their bedroom, and that wasn't for me to worry about. When he gave me these gifts, I felt additional confirmation of his approval. Perhaps he was trying to let me know that I did, after all, find favor in his eyes. I carefully wrapped the cup and the spice holder and put them in my suitcase. Outside, the driver of the cab that was taking me to the airport honked his horn and raced the motor. I hugged my dad, inhaled his musty morning smell, and kissed his stubbled cheek. "Love you, Dad," I said, holding on tightly. "See you in April."

Sometimes I think of my whole life as a search for my father. After my mother left him, my father was a distant presence, physically and in some ways emotionally. For the occasional weekends and Jewish holidays my brothers and I spent with him, Dad would drive in from Hartford in his old Chevy and pick us up at my mother's house in Queens, not lingering for a minute more than absolutely necessary. Those visits to Hartford were important parts of my growing up, but they were ultimately unfulfilling. For no matter how much time I spent with him, the time would come to an end and I would return, fatherless, once again, to my mother.

My yearning for my father carried over from my formative years well into adulthood. When I became old enough to decide for myself how much time I could spend with him, we started disagreeing on my career choice, and that only increased the distance between us. And so I gravitated to men of my father's vintage. I befriended teachers, rabbis, and mentors who reminded me of him. Once, speaking to an unhappily married male friend, Shira referred to "Ari's obsessive attachment" to older men. She mentioned my accountant, my cello teacher, my favorite editor, my favorite rabbi, my literary agent—all of them in their sixties, like my dad. The friend made a sudden and unexpected pass at her. When she rebuffed him, he said, "But Ari's having all these affairs with older men." He missed the point. My attachment was strictly familial.

One of my "older men" was Rabbi Irving Koslowe. He had attended Yeshiva University with my dad and went on to have an unusual career as the Jewish chaplain at the infamous Sing Sing state prison in Ossining, New York. He served there for forty-nine years before his retirement in 1999. (He will forever be known as the rabbi with whom the convicted spies Julius and Ethel Rosenberg spent their final moments before their execution in 1953.) I first met him through journalism—I wrote several stories about him while I was at the *Times*—and later, when I began to teach, he conducted annual tours of the prison for my classes, starting with the Jewish chapel. As it happened, Rabbi Koslowe's retirement party was being held the day after my fiftieth birthday party. Also on that day, my younger brother, Dov, was leaving for Israel to spend the Sukkot holiday with my father. As I was waiting for a friend to pick me up for the drive to Sing Sing, I got a disturbing call from Dov. He said that he had received a cryptic and panicked message from Teme in Israel. "Come quick. Your father is very ill. He may not make it." Dov tried calling her back, but there was no answer.

Dov was at JFK awaiting his flight. I considered not

going to Rabbi Koslowe's party but realized that there was little I could accomplish by staying home. I probably wouldn't know precisely what was going on until Dov landed in Israel some ten hours later, so I went ahead with my trip to Sing Sing. Rabbi Koslowe's party was fun. There was a small ceremony honoring him in the prison chapel, which was named in his honor. Afterward, there was a festive dinner in the correction officers' commissary that was attended by state prison officials and clergy from other faiths.

Throughout all of this, I couldn't shake my uneasy feeling about my father. I tried several times to get information by phone, but no one answered at his home in Jerusalem and none of my Israeli relatives knew what was going on. Dov was in the air, on his way to Israel.

When I got back to my Manhattan apartment that night, the call came. One of my Israeli cousins, David Miller, told me that efforts to revive my father after a massive heart attack had failed. My father was dead. Our immediate concern was to get word to Dov, who was still en route to Israel. We arranged for another cousin, Zalman Deutsch, to meet him at the airport. Dov later told me that when he got off the plane, he was prepared for the worst, and not only because of Teme's phone call. During the previous four years, following the death of our mother, Dov made a point of visiting Israel often. "I must have gone thirteen or fourteen times. I knew Dad didn't have much time left," Dov said. "Every time I said good-bye, I knew it might be the last." A heavy smoker for most of his life, Dad gave up cigarettes and changed his eating habits after suffering a heart attack in 1982. Those reforms, plus Teme's dedicated care, added many good years to his life. But the damage had already been done.

Zalman met Dov at Ben-Gurion Airport and confirmed his fear. Dad had died and the funeral was to be held in a few hours. There was still time, however, to visit the chapel where the *chevra kaddisha,* the members of the burial society, were preparing Dad's body for burial. According to Jewish custom, the body is ritually washed, dressed in hand-sewn white linen shrouds called *tachrichim,* and then wrapped in a *tallit,* or prayer shawl. The final act is to close the eyes of the deceased. While the other functions are performed by the members of the burial society, this final task is carried out, when possible, by a son. It is an act that recalls God's promise to Jacob before his death. "Joseph's hand shall close your eyes," God tells Jacob in Genesis 46:4. Still dazed from the long plane ride and the sad news, Dov arrived in time to perform that final act of filial respect. He washed his hands in the prescribed ritual fashion, pouring water from a cup three times over each hand, and was then led by a rabbi, a member of the burial society, into the room where Dad's body lay wrapped in the burial shrouds.

The shrouds consist of several garments, including a

semicircular cap, known as a *mitznefet,* that covers the head and face. When Dov entered, the *mitznefet* was lifted. Dov shut his eyes; this was just too much for him. The rabbi gently guided Dov's hand to Dad's face, and Dov closed our father's eyes. He was then handed a small bag of earth, taken from the soil of Israel, the contents of which he would sprinkle on Dad's body after it was lowered into the grave. And, finally, he was given pottery shards, which he placed on Dad's eyelids. Dov then repeated the words from the Creation narrative in Genesis 3:19: "For dust you are, and to dust you shall return."

From there, Dov and Zalman drove to Har HaMenu-chot, where a crowd of about a hundred was gathering for the funeral in the hot sun. Moments later the *chevra kad-disha* van arrived. Vans are used rather than hearses in Jerusalem and, following ancient custom, there is no cas-ket. The covered body was carried out on a stretcher and placed on a platform.

Many of our relatives were there, as were my father's *daf yomi* buddies. Dov somehow managed to give an eloquent eulogy. He spoke about return—about how my father returned to the Jewish homeland, which was also the bur-ial place of his father, Samuel H. L. Goldman, and how our grandfather had also come back to Israel at the end of his life. Rabbi Simonson, the *daf yomi* teacher, then spoke, saying that my father had changed the nature of the daily Talmud class by forging friendships and fostering a sense of camaraderie. "Before Marvin Goldman joined us, we were just a Talmud class, but because of Marvin we became a community," he said. Last to speak was one of my uncles.

I always had a warm spot for this particular uncle, but he did not rise to the occasion, at least as far as my brothers and I were concerned. He spoke of his long friendship with my father, which went back more than fifty years. He spoke of my father's youth in Hartford, his career in real estate and his move, seven years earlier, to Israel. He talked about my dad's parents, his love for Teme, and his closeness to his nieces and nephews in Israel. He had nearly finished without so much of a mention of Marvin's sons, until his daughter handed him a note on which she had scribbled "the boys!" And so my uncle concluded his remarks with a somewhat halfhearted nod to his nephews. "And at the end of his life, Marvin was proud of his three sons, Shalom, Ari, and Dov." I like to think that Dad was proud of us all his life, but we were the products of a failed marriage, and having family members occasionally treat us as unpleasant reminders of a regrettable event was something that we were, unfortunately, accustomed to.

After the funeral, the mourners—Teme, my father's sister Ruth, and Dov—went to my father's apartment for an abbreviated *shiva*. With the onset of Sukkot that night, *shiva* was observed for only a few hours. Friends and relatives dropped by to offer words of consolation.

By the time I woke up on Friday morning in New York, the funeral was over in Israel. The night before I had arranged for Ramath Orah's morning *minyan* to meet at my home, some six blocks away on 116th Street, so that I could say *kaddish* during my one day of *shiva*. I also e-mailed several friends with the reference line: "Re: A death in the family." The e-mail distribution list was the same one I had used for my birthday party. How ironic it seemed: One day I ask my friends to join me in celebration, and the next, I call on them to support me in grief.

The *minyan* from Ramath Orah, augmented by family and friends, gathered at my home, surrounding me as I sat on Judah's Little Tikes stool, the lowest chair in our house. Trembling, I rose to say *kaddish* for my father for the first time. After the morning *minyan*, my older brother, Shalom, who had just arrived from his home in Atlanta, joined me. His friends, my friends, and our relatives dropped by for hasty visits. With the arrival of both Shabbat and the Sukkot holiday on Friday night, my *shiva* came to an abrupt end.

The single day of *shiva* for my father was vastly different from the mourning four years earlier for my mother. My mother had died on a Saturday, just a few days after Passover. After the burial on Sunday morning, we sat *shiva* for the full week. According to Jewish law, mourners stay at home during *shiva*, and a variety of pleasures, including listening to music, sexual intercourse, shaving, and wearing leather shoes, are prohibited. As mourners cannot attend synagogue during *shiva,* a *minyan* gathers for morning, afternoon, and evening services in their home. My brothers and I, and my mother's three sisters and brother, all sat *shiva* together, in the home of my aunt Mindy, whose husband, Dr. Norman Lamm, was then president of Yeshiva University.

Hundreds and hundreds of people poured into the Lamms' duplex apartment on Central Park West during the week-long *shiva.* My aunts and uncles all lived in different communities, and people from all these places came to visit, as did old friends from the various neighborhoods in which Shalom, Dov, and I had lived. On some evenings there were so many people in my uncle's commodious living room that it was impossible for a visitor to walk from one end of the room to the other. The *shiva* was loud, long, crowded, and flamboyant, just the kind of event my mother would have appreciated. My father's *shiva* was far more understated and muted: only a handful of friends in my modest apartment in the few hours before *shiva* dissolved into Shabbat and Sukkot. It was a *shiva* my father would have approved of. *"Bacavodick,"* he would have said. "Imbued with honor."

fter the abbreviated *shiva* for my dad, I went to Ramath Orah for the special Friday night service that also welcomed the holiday of Sukkot. With my *shiva* over, I entered *shloshim,* a thirty-day period of mourning (counted from the time of death) that is less intense than *shiva.* Normal life begins to resume for the mourner with the onset of *shloshim.* At the conclusion of *shloshim,* additional restrictions are lifted, and the mourner begins a third, less intense level of mourning, the twelve-month (again, counted from the time of death) period called *aveylut.* The mourner continues to say *kaddish* daily during the first eleven of these months. Customs vary, but I decided that I wouldn't shave or listen to music not only during *shiva,* but through the thirty days of *shloshim* as well.

There are restrictions and obligations that one takes upon oneself and there are others that are imposed by the religious community. For example, it is considered meritorious for a mourner to lead the daily prayer services. But this does not apply on the Sabbath or the festivals, when, because of the joyous nature of the day, it is not considered appropriate for a mourner to lead fellow congregants in prayer. As I entered Ramath Orah that Friday our rabbi,

Steven Friedman, asked me to lead the afternoon service, the last prayer before the beginning of the Sabbath. It was there that I said *kaddish* for the first time with our *shul*'s other mourners. At the conclusion of the service, I stepped down and was replaced by someone else, not in mourning, who began to lead the festival service.

I saw the wisdom of the exclusion of the mourners. I was in no mood to sing. As I headed for my regular seat in the middle of the synagogue, Rabbi Friedman walked over and gently reminded me of another tradition. "During the year of *aveylut*," he said, "you should change your seat in the synagogue." I remembered this tradition; it is one of the ways that the mourner is reminded of his or her loss. But I told the rabbi that this was a tradition I chose not to observe. Feeling vulnerable and bereft of my dad, I knew that I needed the comfort of sitting in my regular seat, near the men I pray with each Sabbath. "I don't think I can handle moving right now," I told him. Rabbi Friedman grasped my arm warmly. "That's okay." He explained that it is only a regional tradition, not a law—an important distinction in rabbinic theology. I could keep my seat.

Sukkot is a joyous seven-day holiday with a good deal of communal praying and eating. The name of the holiday comes from the *sukkot*, or temporary huts, that are built outdoors to re-create the experiences of the Israelites, who journeyed through the desert for forty years, from the liberation from Egypt until their arrival in the Promised Land. Since we live in a Manhattan apartment (without a front or back yard, where *sukkot* are often built), we do not build our own *sukkah*, but take many of our meals in the communal *sukkah* that Ramath Orah builds on its terrace. This meant I was thrust back into community life before I was ready; were it not for Sukkot, I would be allowed to remain home for the balance of the *shiva* week to continue the mourning process. I found this re-immersion difficult—I wasn't really ready yet for the camaraderie and high spirits that went along with eating communal meals with my friends at Ramath Orah's *sukkah*—and I often retreated to our home while Shira and the kids stayed at the synagogue. I knew that everyone understood.

The initial festive days of Sukkot were on Saturday and Sunday. On Monday, I was supposed to resume my normal teaching activities. My *shiva* was technically over but I was acutely aware that I was still in the first week of my loss. I just could not face a room full of students. I canceled class for that week and stayed at home, mostly sitting quietly, alone in my living room, thinking about my dad. Every morning and afternoon, I went to the synagogue to say *kaddish*.

Many friends called during that week to offer their condolences. Letters, notes, and even e-mails about my father began to arrive. (E-mail, which once felt so impersonal and corporate, had suddenly become an acceptable way to express one's emotions.) Every note—no matter how long or short, whether a studio card or a scribbled expression on someone's stationery—arrived like a balm for my pain. Some were simple expressions of sympathy. "We are so sorry to hear of your loss," many wrote. Others were empathic. "My husband lost his father recently, and I know it is one of the great sadnesses of life," one colleague wrote. "You must be in terrible, terrible pain," a student wrote. Some acknowledged that expressions of sympathy were ultimately inadequate, but added: "the knowledge that others care and support you in your grief is a source of some comfort."

One note struck me as ironic, given the relationship I had with my father. A colleague wrote: "I hope you can take some comfort from how proud you must have made your father."

In a handwritten letter, my friend Ike noted how happy I seemed at my fiftieth birthday party, the day before my father's death. "We're never really ready to be without parents," Ike wrote, "but Wednesday night you looked like you could handle anything. I'm sorry that this happened to you but perhaps it's providential that it happened right now." My loss reminded him of the saying: "God never closes a window without opening a door." I'm not sure what God opened and what God closed, but the words were welcome. So were the donations. Many people con-tributed money in my father's memory to their favorite charities and several gave money to mine, to Ramath Orah, where I would spent most of the next year saying *kaddish.*

I so appreciated these condolence notes because I know, firsthand, how hard it is to write them. I have often heard of a death, resolved to send a note, but never did. What can I possibly say? Do they really want to hear from me? What if I say the wrong thing? And what's their address anyway? As a sadly experienced mourner, I now take writing condolence notes far more seriously. I've saved all the letters and e-mails that I received after my mother's and father's passing (in two—separate—shoeboxes). I dip into them sometimes to remember the right thing to say in a condolence note. There's no magic formula, I've found, but the old letters remind me of the importance of saying something.

My week of private mourning at home ended with yet another Jewish festival. The Sukkot holiday concludes with a two-day festival called Shmini Atzeret–Simchat Torah. Shmini Atzeret is one of the four occasions in the Jewish year when a special prayer for the dead called *yizkor* is said. Unlike the rather generic *kaddish, yizkor* is a more personal prayer. The mourner mentions the dead by name, prays for their souls, and pledges charity in their memory. There is a certain drama that surrounds *yizkor* in an Orthodox synagogue, in large part because of a tradition associated with it: only those who have lost immediate family members (parent, sibling, spouse, or child) say *yizkor;* everyone else leaves the synagogue for the duration of the prayer. It is a moment, I always thought, that separates the haves from the have-nots. I'd been a have-not since 1995 when I lost my mother. From that time on, I stayed inside the synagogue for *yizkor.* Now, I realized sadly, I had two reasons to stay. I said *yizkor* for both my mother and my father. But because *yizkor* is gender sensitive (there's one version for men, another for women), the *yizkors* for my mother and father were separate, as I felt they should be. In some synagogues, mine included, *yizkor* ends with a communal recitation of *kaddish.* Far more difficult was saying *kaddish* for the first time for both my mother and my father, in one prayer. Combining my grief for them felt unnatural and forced. I was in mourning for my father; my mother had no place in this *kaddish.* At this point, I could not handle mourning for them both and I welcomed the regular *kaddish* said in the synagogue, a prayer that was said just for my father. This, I knew, was the time to mourn for him.

Weeks earlier, before I lost my father, the president of Ramath Orah, Leo Chester, asked if I would accept the honor of *Chatan B'reshit.* Being *Chatan B'reshit* means that you are called upon to say the very first blessing over the Torah, for the very first *aliyah* on Simchat Torah, the holiday that celebrates the beginning of the year-long cycle of weekly Torah readings, which starts with Genesis—in Hebrew, *B'reshit.* The word *chatan* means bridegroom. The *Chatan B'reshit,* is in effect, escorting the Torah, often personified in Jewish tradition as a bride, to the new cycle of reading. It seemed an especially appropriate honor, Mr. Chester said, because it has become my personal tradition to read that portion of Genesis each year in the synagogue. (*B'reshit* was my bar mitzvah portion, learned thirty-seven years earlier and never forgotten.)

Suddenly thrust into the category of a mourner, I was not sure that it actually was an appropriate honor. How could I be a bridegroom of anything at a time like this? I checked with Rabbi Friedman and found that there was no technical restriction. "It's up to you," he said. I remembered that my dad was particularly pleased that I kept reading my bar mitzvah portion each year. He asked me about it every year when he called for my birthday. I decided that to go ahead with being called to the Torah as the *Chatan B'reshit* would be to honor his memory.

The synagogue was filled to capacity on Simchat Torah, which is a popular holiday among Jews on Manhattan's Upper West Side and also brings many visitors to the neighborhood. Ramath Orah gets more worshipers on

Simchat Torah than it does on Yom Kippur, the holiest and most solemn day of the year.

The mood was joyous as I rose to lead the congregation in beginning the new cycle of Torah reading. All around me it was Simchat Torah, but in my heart it was Yom Kippur.

4

I go to an Orthodox *shul*—that is where I feel most at home—but I am not conventionally Orthodox, especially by today's standards. I like to think of myself as 1950s Orthodox, harkening back to an era when Orthodoxy was a big tent, an identity, not an absolute list of behaviors. This was before the arrival of two countervailing trends in American Judaism. In the next generation, Orthodoxy would begin to move sharply to the right, powered by the wave of fervently Orthodox Eastern European refugees from Hitler's Europe. At the same time, alternatives to Orthodoxy became more accessible as Jews moved out of the inner cities and away from their local Orthodox *shuls,* settling in the suburbs, where they built Conservative and Reform synagogues that more closely reflected their religious practices.

I decided long ago that I would cling to Orthodoxy, even as it shifted under my feet. I'd rather be the bad boy of Orthodoxy, I figured, than the *tzaddik* of Conservative Judaism. I have written extensively about this in magazine articles and in my earlier books. The mail I get confirms that there are many Orthodox Jews whose practice parallels mine; they just don't talk about it.

But despite all of this, I am happiest in an Orthodox

synagogue, praying among men. While I can see the logic of the Conservative and Reform belief that men and women should, in fact, pray together, I find wisdom in the Orthodox separation of men and women for prayer. There are times when I prefer to be with men. Another one of these times is at my men's group, which meets monthly at the homes of our members. I organized the group, which we call the *tertulia,* with my friends Jack Nelson and Enrique Levy a year before my father's death, as an informal forum to discuss issues that we care deeply about, such as religion and politics and sexuality. Each of us brought in a handful of friends, and at any given meeting we have about ten men—not for prayer, just for discussion. Enrique was the one who gave it its name. As a boy growing up in Cuba, he remembered the men going off to their *tertulias,* a males-only social club, to talk. A *tertulia* was scheduled for the evening of October 5, just eleven days after my father's death. I was looking forward to it. Denied a full *shiva,* I hoped to be able to share what I was feeling at this gathering of good friends.

As I was getting ready to leave for the *tertulia,* the phone rang. It was my aunt Bracha, one of my mother's sisters. "I have sad news," she said. "Aunt Minnie just died. Can you come right over?" I called my *tertulia* mates to tell them that I wasn't coming and I took a cab to Aunt Minnie's apartment, thirty blocks away on West Eighty-sixth

Street. I rode the elevator to the second floor, as I had done hundreds of times since I was a little boy.

Aunt Minnie was my great-aunt, and she was 105 when she died in her own home. In accordance with Jewish law, her body had been placed on the floor, head to the door, and covered with a sheet. A few inches away from her head, my aunt Bracha had placed a lit candle. Earlier that night, Fanny, her home health aide, had served Aunt Minnie dinner at the kitchen table and then sat her down in her wheelchair in the dining room. Fanny was cleaning up when Aunt Minnie called her to her side. "Fanny," she said, "you're very good to me. God bless you. Thank you." Then she turned to the side, closed her eyes, and was gone.

Those final words could have been her epitaph. Aunt Minnie died as she lived, with the name of God on her lips and thanks in her heart. She was a major religious influence on my life and my decision to remain Orthodox, albeit in my own way. In some ways she was like a second mother to me. Her death, coming so soon after my father's, was a terrible hurt.

But the double blow was felt only by my brothers and me. My mother's family did not join in the mourning for my father; it mattered little to them. And that hurt, too.

Aunt Minnie was the eldest of three sisters, all with turn-of-the-last-century names: Minnie, Tillie, and Paulie. When my brothers and I were growing up, that matriarchal triumvirate dominated our lives. Ours was a working mother, long before it became fashionable. After my parents divorced my mother took a teaching job, but it was not for personal fulfillment or career advancement—it was to help put food on the table. Enter the triumvirate. Grandma Tillie cooked blintzes, Aunt Minnie made chicken, and Aunt Paulie made desserts. They shipped them over to us in Queens with visiting aunts and uncles. ("You driving? Drop this off for Judy and the boys," they'd say to whoever had stopped by, handing them a package.) And we spent a lot of time with them, first in Brooklyn and later in Manhattan.

I most vividly remember Minnie and Paulie's Manhattan apartments, first on 111th Street and later on Eighty-sixth Street, where they lived among dark carpets and overstuffed furniture. The centerpiece of their living room was a pale blue silk couch with wooden trim and huge cushions; every time you sat on it, there was a great indentation. The aunts had enormous patience with this couch (and with us); they puffed it up after each seating. But we could sit there as much as we wanted. There were no "off limits" at Minnie and Paulie's. We could help ourselves to the goodies in the refrigerator (as long as we said a blessing, or *b'racha*, before eating) and we knew where the dominoes and the marbles were kept (in the top drawer of the telephone table in the hallway). Aunt Paulie was always up for a game, a dance, or a joke.

I slept in Aunt Paulie's room, on a cozy portable bed

with a thin mattress that she usually kept folded up in the closet. Before I went to sleep, she would show me how to fold my clothes and put them on a chair so they'd be ready for morning. When I woke, Aunt Minnie, her head covered with a *tichel,* would be slowly making her way through the morning prayers in a Hebrew prayerbook that had Yiddish translations. The kitchen table was pushed up against a radiator that was next to a window. From that wonderful perch, my aunts would talk to me about the world outside, teaching me to fear it a little bit but also how to conquer it.

The garbage men would come in their enormous trash-gobbling and smoke-spewing truck, clanging the metal cans in front of each building before moving on to the next. "Go to school, or you'll be a garbage man," Aunt Minnie would exclaim. A man would walk by with a bad limp. "Drink your milk or you too will be a cripple." Such were the lessons of my youth.

When Minnie and Paulie lived on 111th Street they prayed at Ramath Orah. I have vague memories of sitting with them on Shabbat in the women's balcony when I was ten or eleven, and still young enough to be allowed to sit with the women. I would look down at the action below in the men's section, thinking how vast the *shul* seemed.

Ramath Orah's great domed ceiling rises five stories high. A long stage dominates the front of the room. In the center of the stage is the holy ark, which holds the Torah scrolls, swathed in red and blue velvet covers and crowned with silver. Immediately above the ark are two great tablets with gold-leaf lettering representing the Ten Commandments. And above that is the organ loft, a remnant of the days when Ramath Orah was a Unitarian church. In four sections at either side of the organ loft are the exposed gold-leaf organ pipes—fifty-two in all, ranging from four feet to twelve feet tall. Upstairs, the women's gallery wraps around three sides of the *shul*. There are stained-glass windows at the rear. In shades of blue and green, they depict an eagle, a crown, a lion, and other symbols set against Jewish stars. The windows are dedicated to people and by people long gone. One window is reserved for the memory of the six million Jews who died at the hands of the Nazis.

Ramath Orah was founded in 1942 by Jewish refugees from Luxembourg, the tiny European nation—no bigger than Rhode Island—sandwiched among Belgium, France, and Germany. In 1940, Luxembourg had a population of roughly 400,000—of whom 5,000 were Jews, many of them prosperous businessmen. The leader of the Jewish community was Rabbi Robert Serebrenik, a handsome and urbane Austrian, who held a doctorate in political science from the University of Vienna. Using his connections and money that he raised, Rabbi Serebrenik managed to shepherd virtually all the Jews out of the country as Hitler rose to power in neighboring Germany. Even after May 10, 1940, when the German army invaded The Netherlands, Belgium, and Luxembourg, Rabbi Serebrenik met with German officials—including the notorious Adolf Eichmann—to secure visas and transit for Jews to France, Portugal, and Spain. He later testified as a prosecution witness at Eichmann's trial in Jerusalem.

In June 1941, Rabbi Serebrenik arrived in New York with sixty-six other refugees from his community. Together with a handful of Luxembourg Jews already here, he established the "Luxembourg Committee for the Organization of Services on the High Holidays 1941." The organization went on to form Congregation Ramath Orah a year later. The name is a translation into Hebrew of the country of their origin. *Lux* is light in Latin, which is *orah* in Hebrew. *Bourg,* which means mountain in German, is *ramath* in Hebrew. Hence, Ramath Orah, or the Light on the Hill, or Luxembourg. The congregation leased the 110th Street property from the American Unitarian Association, and when the lease ran out in 1945, they raised enough money to buy the building from the Unitarians.

In the 1950s and 1960s, Ramath Orah had more than 200 members, a Hebrew School, and adult education classes. In addition to the rabbi, there was a staff of four and numerous volunteer committees. But then the neighborhood began to change, the younger members moved away, and there was no one to replace the founders as they began to die off. By the late 1980s, Ramath Orah was just a shadow of its former self. Membership dwindled, money was scarce, and the handful of regulars looked angrily inward, turning their backs on the world outside. Many Jewish Columbia University students from that era remember Ramath Orah as a large, barren, and unfriendly place. It even smelled old and musty. "The mildew *shul*," one friend remembered. The people who ran it were wizened and bitter.

With the upturn of the New York economy in the 1990s and the rejuvenation of the Columbia area and later neighboring Harlem, Ramath Orah started a long climb back to stability. When I moved into the neighborhood in 1994, the morning *minyan* was being kept alive by the efforts of one man, Manfred Tauber, a Polish Holocaust survivor, who drove around the neighborhood each morning in his Ford Taurus, picking up many of the ten men needed for prayers. On some mornings, I remember standing outside the synagogue with Mr. Tauber, looking for that tenth man, but most of those who passed by our doors were African Americans or Puerto Ricans. In those days, there were even Friday nights when we had trouble getting a *minyan* for the Sabbath service. On Saturday mornings, we'd have thirty people, a depressing pittance for a synagogue built for twelve times that many.

My wife, the daughter of a Conservative rabbi, wanted to go elsewhere. We tried other *shuls,* such as the one at the nearby Jewish Theological Seminary, the academic center of Conservative Judaism, and Ansche Chesed, a popular egalitarian congregation that has experienced its own revival in recent years. But I was drawn to Ramath Orah. It was a bit depressing at times, but it reminded me of home. I believed it could be made better. And besides, our children seemed most happy there. There were one or two other families with children their ages, and there was a vast social hall, where the kids could play. We joined the *shul* (although my wife is happier praying at Ansche Chesed) and I was asked to join the board. Within a couple of years, I found myself vice president.

By the late 1990s, the *shul* had fewer than eighty-five members (many of them unable to pay the full dues of $350 a year), so the idea of hiring a full-time rabbi was out of the question. But beginning in 1996, as the area around Columbia was rejuvenated, the *shul* began to bring in rabbis and rabbinical students, who turned things around. Rabbi Jeffrey Kobrin, whose fine sermons drew on his Yeshiva University education and Columbia University English degree, brought students back to the *shul* in large numbers. When Rabbi Kobrin left after a year to spend time in Israel, the *shul* hired Steven Friedman as "acting rabbi," a term we used because he was not actually a rabbi, but a lawyer. (He was later ordained.) Steven was working at a white-shoe law firm downtown, but he longed to put his passion for Judaism to good use by working with a congregation. He succeeded in knitting together into one community the students who had wandered into Ramath Orah and the old-timers who had been there for decades. The *shul* also hired two "rabbinic interns" from Yeshiva University, Barry Wimpheimer and Shamir Caplan. Barry and Shamir wanted to introduce the charismatic "Carlebach" style of prayer to Ramath Orah for Friday night services, but the old-time members of the board resisted the idea of instituting the lengthy singing and dancing form of worship that had been created by the late Jewish folksinger Rabbi Shlomo Carlebach. And they were even less enthusiastic about Barry and Shamir's other suggestion: to divide the main sanctuary evenly between men and women by placing the *mechitza* down the center of the synagogue, so that women would no longer be relegated to the distant balcony. After much negotiation, a compromise was reached. The old-style service would be held in the main sanctuary and the Carlebach service would be held downstairs in the social hall, which was divided in half with a portable *mechitza* that Barry and Shamir built themselves.

The Carlebach service proved to be enormously popular, and it grew as the *minyan* in the main sanctuary shriveled. Even opponents of the Carlebach service went downstairs to see what all the commotion was about. Within weeks, resistance crumbled and the Carlebach service moved upstairs together with the makeshift *mechitza.* With the sanctuary floor now evenly divided between men and women, Ramath Orah joined the small handful of "progressive" Orthodox synagogues. The transition did not take place overnight. At first, the portable *mechitza* was used only on Friday nights; on Saturday mornings the women returned to the balcony. But after almost a year, the change was complete. The *mechitza* down the middle stayed.

With the new *mechitza* firmly in place, the Friday night service grew and grew. There would be 200 men on one side of the room and 200 women on the other side, all singing their hearts out. Denominational affiliation did not seem to matter. While Orthodox Columbia students predominated, rabbinical students from the Conservative Jewish Theological Seminary and the Reform Hebrew Union College-Jewish Institute of Religion also came in large numbers. Even the chancellor of the Jewish Theological Seminary, the de facto head of the Conservative movement, became a regular Friday night worshiper. On some nights, there were so many worshipers that the sanctuary was full and we had to use the balcony, which was then divided: one side for men and the other for women. Aunt Minnie and Aunt Paulie would have gotten quite a kick out of it, I think.

5

While several hundred men and women would come on Friday night and Saturday morning, the *shul* still struggled on weekdays to pull together a daily morning *minyan*. The Orthodox Columbia students had their own daily *minyan,* as did the students at the Jewish Theological Seminary. What's more, ours was the earliest service, meeting at 7:00 A.M., an hour rather unattractive to most students.

It's a rather unattractive hour for me as well, but the obligation to say *kaddish* is a strong motivator. It got me out of bed shortly after 6:00 A.M. and out the door by 6:50, for the ten-minute walk to *shul.* The *New York Times* would be there on my doorstep, but I'd have to steel myself and walk right over it if I was to be on time. I wouldn't even look at the headlines. Leaving at that hour also took the forbearance and cooperation of my wife, who had to get our three children off to school by 7:40 without my help.

Walking to *shul* through the early morning streets of upper Manhattan was eerie, a far cry from the hustle and bustle that would envelop the neighborhood in a few hours. In the minutes before 7:00 A.M., traffic was still light. Construction workers holding steaming cups of cof-

fee would gather in small clusters in front of one Columbia building or another that was going up or under reno-
vation. A runner on his way to Riverside Park would jog
past. A woman in sweatpants and looking barely awake
would be walking her German shepherd. Nurses in white
shoes and doctors in their scrubs would be arriving for the
early shift at St. Luke's Hospital on 113th Street. A homeless
man would be looking through a wire mesh garbage can
on the corner for empty bottles and cans. I'd walk under
the shadow of the Cathedral of St. John the Divine and
then cross Amsterdam Avenue to get a whiff of the crois-
sants baking at the neighborhood hangout, the Hungarian
Pastry Shop. The shop was not yet open, but an employee
would be putting out the plastic chairs and tables for the
regulars who would soon be meeting at the shop's sidewalk café for breakfast. I'd give a quarter to a beggar on the
corner of 110th and Amsterdam and then head toward
Broadway to the *shul* entrance.

It seemed that no matter what time I got to *shul*, Dr.
James Schmeidler was already there. In his late fifties,
married and with three children, Dr. Schmeidler is a statistician in the psychiatry department at Mount Sinai Hospital across town on the East Side. He'd open the *shul*
every morning at 6:45, switch on the lights, take his seat in
the sanctuary, and begin to pray while waiting for everyone else to arrive. Dr. Schmeidler wasn't a fellow *kaddish-*

sayer. He lived on West Eighty-third Street, quite a distance away from Ramath Orah, and he came to our *minyan* because a friend of his, one of our board members, told him we needed help in coming up with the ten men that were required. He got there so early, he told me, because he prayed slowly and needed a head start on everyone else.

Dr. Schmeidler was not born Orthodox. He was raised by secular Jewish parents and discovered religion while attending Columbia, where he was invited by a Hasidic rabbi to spend a weekend in Crown Heights, the world headquarters of the Lubavitch Hasidim. He decided to approach the weekend as a scientist. "Since I'm a statistician, statistical experimental ways of doing things are congenial to me," he said. During the weekend, he was told about the 613 Jewish ritual observances, called *mitzvot*, that are outlined in the Torah. Observing them, he was told, would make his life better. "What I said to myself was, try to do *mitzvot* and see what happens." He gave me as an example Sabbath observance. "I discovered that keeping Shabbos in the traditional Orthodox fashion really did create a day of rest. My interpretation is that while you tell yourself not to turn on the light, not to tear the toilet paper, not to, not to, not to, you also tell yourself, 'don't worry about all the other things you worry about the other six days of the week.' And being able to turn off what you're worried about, makes it a day of rest. Now, if you didn't have all these negatives, you probably wouldn't be able to do it."

"I'm an empiricist," he concluded. "I experimented and it worked for me." I was intrigued. Here I was, born into Orthodoxy and struggling all my life to come to terms with what it expected of me, and here was someone who had voluntarily taken on all of its stringencies and obligations. He was also far more at peace with it. I struggled.

I tried to draw Dr. Schmeidler into a theological conversation about revelation and obligation. What about God? Does God want us to do *mitzvot*? Do we do *mitzvot* because we are commanded to do them or because they "work" for us?

Dr. Schmeidler clearly didn't want to go there. He had found a warm embrace in the Orthodox world and raised his three children in it (they're all Orthodox). He admitted to having some disagreements with some aspects of Orthodoxy but said he was drawn more to observance than theology. "Then it's a pragmatic choice for you," I suggested. "That's a good way of putting it," he replied.

6

The other dependable *shul* early bird was Allan Kozinn, who would usually be walking in when I got there. Like Dr. Schmeidler he was a *ba'al teshuva*, a "returnee" to observant Judaism, but one who had taken a very different journey. Allan is a classical music critic for the *New York Times* and four or five nights a week reviews concerts in places such as Carnegie Hall and Avery Fisher Hall, as well as music festivals outside of New York City, such as Tanglewood, Aspen, Santa Fe, and Marlboro. He's also regarded as one of the foremost American authorities on the Beatles.

Allan and I overlapped only briefly at the *Times*. He started as a freelance critic in 1988 but by the time he was hired full-time in 1991, I was already thinking about leaving the paper. I had been there since 1973 and I eventually left in 1993 to teach full-time at Columbia. The one time Allan and I remember meeting each other was at a "Polish Tea Room" lunch organized by Richard F. Shepard, one of my *New York Times* mentors. Richard, a marvelous journalist, was the unofficial social director of the newsroom. He'd organize these lunches at the down-at-the-heels Edison Café on West Forty-sixth Street as a way to get people out of the newsroom and to introduce reporters, editors, clerks, and secretaries from different departments to one another. I came from metropolitan news and Allan from culture. In a place as big as the *Times* we could work in the same building for years and never meet.

Allan, born in 1954, grew up in New York's Westchester County, where his family attended an Orthodox synagogue and he went to afterschool Hebrew classes. His family was very culturally Jewish but not terribly observant of the day-to-day rituals. Allan recalls rushing home from synagogue on Saturday mornings to watch Beatles cartoons on television—not an Orthodox thing to do. After his bar mitzvah, Allan stayed on for one extra year of Hebrew school but then drifted away from synagogue and religion. When his father died in 1990, he returned home to sit *shiva* with his mother, sister, and brother but did not say *kaddish* for his father beyond the *shiva* period. In the year after losing his father, however, his interest in Judaism was sparked by an unusual source. Allan, an early e-mail user, got into a heavy on-line discussion about religion with a fundamentalist Christian in Arkansas, who was bent on converting him. Their discussion, Allan told me, went back and forth almost nightly for a year and consisted of some 600 e-mails. At first, Allan answered his interlocutor from his own knowledge of Judaism. Then, he started reading, buying books from a local Jewish bookstore to bone up on Jewish theology and ritual practice. He held the fundamentalist at bay, but felt that he needed to know—and experience—more as a Jew. He looked for a nearby synagogue and found Ramath Orah, one block away from his home on 111th Street.

Allan began attending our morning *minyan* because going only on Saturdays didn't seem like enough. "I tend to take a black and white view of things," he told me years later. "Either you don't believe in it and you don't go—and you don't do *kashrut* and you don't do Shabbos—or you do believe in it and part of believing in it is that you're required to pray." Allan sometimes felt that he was better able to concentrate on his praying at home, alone, but he showed up every morning for the *minyan,* anyway.

"I think one of the reasons I go to the *minyan*," he said, "is that the system to which I have belatedly subscribed suggests that that's the best thing to do. And more than that, other people who go there believe that it's necessary, and if I'm going to be praying anyway, I might as well go and make it possible for others to have a *minyan.*" His main concern was that there would be a *minyan* for the people who needed it the most—mourners like me.

As Allan became more and more observant, he faced some of the same issues that I faced as an Orthodox reporter for the *Times.* Newspapers, being seven-day-a-week operations, have little sympathy for Sabbath observers. While your editor says, "stay with the story," your tradition tells you, "Shabbos is coming. Stop working Friday at sundown." Each of us navigated this conflict in his own way. I moved out of the hard news—constantly breaking stories such as fires and local crime—and into religion reporting, which afforded me more flexibility. It also meant that I had to work on Sundays—usually covering Cardinal John O'Connor, the archbishop of New York, at St. Patrick's Cathedral—and so I was off on Fridays. Likewise, Allan arranged to be off on Thursday and Friday nights. He works on Saturday nights, but usually only after sundown, which is when most concerts start, anyway.

Allan had a *kaddish* story of his own, too. He had been attending our morning *minyan* for a year when a neighbor and friend, Deborah Norden, died in an airplane crash near Pittsburgh. At the memorial service he learned that no one would be saying *kaddish* for her because her parents were not observant and her husband considered himself a Buddhist. Allan felt that someone should remember Deborah with a year-long *kaddish,* and so he assumed the obligation himself. Most of all, he was moved by the death of this young woman who had been his friend. But, as he also told me, "In the back of my mind was that I could in some way perhaps make up for not saying *kaddish* for my father."

Where did he get the idea? He said that he was following the example of a friend of his father's named Archie

Green. When Archie realized that Allan and his brother would not be saying the year-long *kaddish* for their father, he decided to take on the obligation himself in memory of his friend. "I did for Deborah what Archie did for my father," Allan said. And several years later, when Archie died and left no one to say *kaddish*, Allan Kozinn spent another year saying *kaddish*, at Ramath Orah, this time for Archie Green.

7

Along with divorce came stepparents. My parents were single for many years after their divorce and didn't remarry until I was a young adult—my mother when I was twenty, my father when I was twenty-four. I was happy that they both enjoyed successful second marriages, and their spouses were rather positive influences on my life. Most important, they kept my parents happy and secure, right up to the times of their deaths. In both cases, the loyalty and love of their spouses enriched and in some ways lengthened my mother's and father's lives. But stepparents are another legacy of divorce. What was my relationship to them once my parents were gone? And what about my parents' possessions? My stepparents were the legal heirs, but what was my brothers' and my inheritance?

The one thing of my mother's that I really wanted was the three-pronged sterling silver candelabra she lit every Friday night to usher in the Sabbath. I remember watching her light it when I was a boy, and I wanted it on my Sabbath table. Jack, my stepfather, resisted at first, but eventually he had to acknowledge that my mother did have the candelabra before they were married and that it now belonged to her children. My brothers, without families of their own at the time, agreed to let me have it. And when Shira lights it every Friday night I feel my mother's presence.

The one thing of my father's that I really wanted was his *tallit*. It was a big woolen broadsheet of a prayer shawl with beefy, thick *tzitzit* at the corners. When you gathered up the four corners of this *tallit* for the *sh'ma* prayer in which you proclaimed your belief in one God, you held something substantial in your hand. The *tallit* had an *atara,* or mantle, around the shoulders that was made of sterling silver. Teme immediately agreed that I, as the one married son, should have the *tallit.* When Dov returned from Israel after Sukkot, he brought it with him. It arrived in my father's blue velvet *tallit* bag. The next morning in *shul,* I took the *tallit* out of the bag, stood tall, and wrapped it around my shoulders and over my head. Under Dad's *tallit,* for the first time since his death, I allowed myself to cry—big, heaving, private sobs. My feet buckled and I sat in my pew, alone with my sadness. At one and the same time, I felt my father's lingering presence and his gaping absence. It was the same *tallit* that he gathered my brothers and me under during the priestly blessing when we went to *shul* with him as kids. But now I was underneath the *tallit* by myself. When I took it off, I put it not into my father's *tallit* bag, but into my own.

Dov and I sat down a few days later to assess our inheritance. While I got the *tallit*, he got my father's handwritten Scroll of Esther. Shalom got my father's *tefillin*, the phylacteries he wore daily during prayer, and some sacred books.

8

When I started saying *kaddish* in September 1999, I was the lone mourner at Ramath Orah. To be sure, there were others saying *kaddish,* but they were not technically required to do so. They were saying *kaddish,* in effect voluntarily, for other relatives—grandparents, aunts, uncles—and some were saying *kaddish* for friends. The only person *required* to say *kaddish* is a child for a parent. Where there are no children, another close relative—spouse, sibling, grandchild, parent—may assume the responsibility, but it is not required.

Kaddish, an Aramaic poem that praises God, is one of the oldest parts of the synagogue liturgy. It is also one of the most powerful and most enduring. Dating back to the first century, it was probably recited in the very first synagogues established after the destruction of the Second Temple in Jerusalem in the year 70 C.E. The central lines of *kaddish* are mentioned in the Talmud, which was written and edited in the third to the sixth centuries. The early rabbinic sources show *kaddish* associated with the study of sacred texts—it was said at the conclusion of Torah study—but by the Middle Ages, it became linked with mourning. At a certain point in the synagogue service, the head of the congregation would go outside where the mourners sat and say *kaddish* for them. Later, it was the mourners themselves who led the prayer. In his book *When a Jew Dies,* Samuel C. Heilman writes that saying *kaddish* publicly "turns this prayer from a sterile mourner's monologue into a dialogue of praise of life." Rabbi Maurice Lamm, the author of *The Jewish Way in Death and Mourning,* calls *kaddish* "a self-contained, miniature service that achieves the heights of holiness."

At a time of great loss, the natural inclination is to question, rebel, reject, and diminish God. But the tradition calls on the mourner not merely to praise God, but to lead others in this ancient praise poem. *"Yitkadal veyitkadash sh'mei rabah,"* it begins. "May His great name grow exalted and sanctified forever and ever." *Kaddish* was written in Aramaic, the lingua franca of Talmudic times, so that it would be understandable to all. Today, the Aramaic means little to most Jews, but the words and rhythms and alternating responses of *kaddish* retain their emotional power. Whenever I visit a Reform congregation, I am struck by the fact that *kaddish* is still said in Aramaic, even though almost every other prayer is said in English.

The obligation to say *kaddish* also thrusts the mourner out of his or her home and into the community at a time when it might be easier to withdraw and quietly grieve. Community has therapeutic properties. Rabbi Lamm notes that, as a practical matter, *kaddish* has served several purposes. "The recitation of *kaddish* has united the gen-

erations in a vertical chain"—from parent to child—
"while the requirement to gather the *minyan* for *kaddish*
has united Jews on the horizontal plane," he writes. *Kaddish* binds the mourner to the past and the present.

Contrary to what one might expect, *kaddish* makes no
explicit mention of the dead. The prayer begins with an
acknowledgment of God's rule over the earth "as He
willed." We may not understand God's will—especially at
a time of loss—but we submit to it even when it goes
against our very nature. *Kaddish* continues with a plea
for the ultimate redemption—the messianic era—when
God's kingdom will be recognized by all. Addressing the
congregation, the mourner prays that the redemption will
come about "in your lifetimes and in your days and in the
lifetimes of the entire family of Israel, swiftly and soon."
The congregation replies with the words: "May His great
name grow exalted and sanctified forever and ever," a
phrase that is then repeated by the mourner. The call and
response of *kaddish*—in effect, the public acknowledgment of ultimate faith in God—is so essential to the
prayer that *kaddish* can be said only as part of public
prayer, in a *minyan* made up of ten worshipers, all of
whom reply with a loud "amen" at five specific points.

Kaddish has a few different forms and variations, but all
have these essential elements: Aramaic, call and response,
praise of God, submission to God's will, and hope for
redemption. A special *kaddish* is said at the graveside after

burial. Two other variations, called *Half Kaddish* and *Full Kaddish*, are said during the synagogue service by the person leading the prayers. The *Mourner's Kaddish* and the *Rabbi's Kaddish* are reserved for the mourners. In its various forms, *kaddish* is said several times during each of the three daily services. In any of its variations, it rarely takes more than a minute to recite. The *Mourner's Kaddish*, for example, is just seventy-five words long. But despite its brevity, it is one of the most poignant prayers in the liturgy.

The most powerful story associated with *kaddish* is the legend of Rabbi Akiva, which is examined at great length—and from every angle—in Leon Weiseltier's book, *Kaddish.* The story has Rabbi Akiva, the great Talmudic sage, walking past a cemetery late at night and seeing an apparition, his complexion black as coal, carrying a load of wood "heavy enough for ten men." Rabbi Akiva orders the man to stop. "Why do you do such hard work?" Rabbi Akiva asks.

"Do not detain me lest my masters be angry with me," the spirit responds. "I am a dead man. Every day I am punished anew by being sent to chop wood for a fire in which I am consumed."

"What did you do in your life?"

"I was a tax collector," the spirit responds. "I would be lenient with the rich and oppress the poor."

"Have you heard if there is any way to save you?"

The spirit responds that his only salvation would be if he had a son who would say *kaddish* and have the congregation respond: "May His great name grow exalted and sanctified forever and ever."

As the spirit disappears into the night, Rabbi Akiva resolves to find the man's family. He journeys to the man's town and inquires about the much-hated tax collector. The townspeople curse the man's name but point Rabbi Akiva to an ignorant and illiterate lad, the accursed man's son. Rabbi Akiva takes the boy under his wing, teaches him to pray, and eventually brings him to the synagogue, where he says the *kaddish* prayer. The congregation responds: "May His great name grow exalted and sanctified forever and ever."

That night, the tortured soul appears to Rabbi Akiva in a dream, blesses him, and tells him that he has been released from his eternal punishment.

Weiseltier concludes: "The themes of the story? That the dead are in need of spiritual rescue; and that the agent of that spiritual rescue is the son; and that the instrument of spiritual rescue is prayer, notably *kaddish*."

The message? We, the living, cannot bring back the dead, but we can redeem death. God's will is done, but so is ours.

And so we say *kaddish,* which serves, in Heilman's lovely phrase, "like a bell tolling morning and evening, the reminder that life has changed."

9

In the weeks after my father died, I wait to hear from him. Maybe it had to do with the fact that he had been living in Israel for seven years and we were not in daily contact. Because of our strained relationship, even when he lived in the States, he was always a somewhat distant presence in my life. We would sometimes go for weeks without being in touch. Dad's not dead, I told myself, just busy. He's bound to call or e-mail any day now. In the last years of his life, my father discovered the Internet and became a great devotee. He'd use it for his Torah study, looking up sources and joining on-line discussions. He'd also share Torah insights, jokes, and simple greetings with me, and others, on e-mail. At one point, my friend Julie Triedman, a freelance writer who teaches with me at Columbia, was working on an article for the *Times'* Circuits section about the Talmud and the Internet. I put her in touch with my father and they had a great long-distance conversation. Dad told her about the Web-sites he visited and how he shared what he learned with his *daf yomi* class. The interview went well until Julie asked if she could use his name. I could have predicted the response. "I'm not that important," he'd say. "Don't use my name." Of course, newspapers like to use names and without one, my father didn't make it into the article.

Dad's nature was to be self-effacing. How I wish I had that clip now, with his quotes, here in my hands. Maybe the *Times* would have even taken a picture of him. He was that important.

I don't have that article, but I do have dozens of e-mail messages from him that I saved over four years in a separate computer file called "Dad." It's remarkable how they capture his voice and his spirit. He wrote in a clipped, formal manner curiously spiced with puns, wonder, and humor. "Looking forward to this new mode of communicating," he said about e-mail, in a note dated October 26, 1995. "Anxious to know that you received this." He wrote about desktops and laptops and software he'd received and the joy of using them. "We just received an updated Netscape called Netscape Navigator with a guidebook that really helps." He continually sent articles, Torah thoughts, and updates on his health. When he wrote about his health, he did so with a detached, almost lawyerlike tone. "Yesterday I had a re-evaluation by the pain clinic physician and will resume reflexology treatment, which is not necessarily a long-range *refuah* [cure] but gives some relief."

On April 11, 1999, a few days before the surgery to remove the cancer discovered in his lung, he wrote that he is a good candidate for the operation because the cancer is in one place and not distributed throughout the lung. "The important fact," he added, "is the monitoring of the heart during the procedure."

On May 27, 1999—four months before he passed away—he wrote with a touch of humor about his recovery from the April surgery. "*Hakol beseder* [All is in order]," he began. "Gradually—Yiddle by Yiddle—returning to somewhat of a normal routine—except for rude awakenings during the night, trying to find my position in life. Good news is that I'm out daily and, in fact, doing some driving locally."

That is the last e-mail I have from him. From that point on, his condition began to deteriorate, and I guess he was just too tired to log on.

Even as I said *kaddish* for him every day, I somehow still found it hard to believe that I would never again receive another e-mail from my father. And I know that if there were some way to send electronic messages from heaven, Dad would be the first to do it.

In the late fall, a month after Dad died, I was visiting my in-laws in Forest Hills, Queens, with my family. It had been windy and raining heavily, but soon after we got to their house, the rain stopped. While Shira and Adam stayed in the house to visit with Shira's parents, I took Emma and Judah to the running track behind Forest Hills High School, about a block away. I stopped at our car to pick up some rubber balls and an old kite that I kept for just such occasions. We played in the relatively dry grassy area at the center of the track and tried to avoid the running areas, some of which were deeply rutted and were like little ponds, filled with water.

We played catch, at least as best you can with one fifty-year-old, one eleven-year-old, and one four-year-old. First one ball rolled into one of the ruts, then another, and then a third. "Let's fly our kite," I suggested. I held the string and Emma the tail, and soon the kite was aloft. When I looked back at the ground, I saw Judah, fifty feet away, tottering at the edge of one of the ruts, trying to retrieve one of our lost balls with a stick. "C-A-R-E-F-U-L," I shouted. Judah stopped suddenly, and stared at me. I guess I had never screamed that loud. And I too stopped and listened to the echo, because it was not my voice. It was the cry of my father. I had been waiting to hear from him. But the message did not come via the telephone or through e-mail. It came from deep inside me.

10

I had very different relationships with my mother and father, and so mourning for each of them was different. When my mother died in 1995, I said *kaddish* for her for the year, but that was just one element of my grieving. I was closer to my mother. She raised me and was always there for me. A good mother is a fact of life, like the sun coming up each morning. When she died, it seemed as though the sun had stopped shining. In accordance with the traditional laws of mourning, I did not go to hear live music for the year after her death. Hearing a live performance—whether in a concert hall or the park or at a wedding or bar mitzvah—is considered a festive occasion, both because of the music and the simple joy of being with others. It is no place for mourners. But in mourning for my mother, I took the music restriction even one step further. I did not even listen to music on the radio or on CDs. And I put away the doleful cello music that I loved so well. Music, even sad music, has always lifted my spirits, and I did not want my spirits to be lifted. I needed to feel the loss of my mother. Another restriction is not to buy new clothing for a year. New clothes also bring one joy. And I wanted neither clothes nor joy.

Mourning for my father, however, focused on prayer. My relationship with him in large measure centered on the synagogue. As a young boy I spent mostly Saturdays and Jewish holidays with him, days largely spent in *shul.* We went twice a day, morning and evening. And my father liked to get there early; he didn't want to miss a prayer. I learned Hebrew in school, but it was my dad who taught me how to pray. From him I learned the rhythm and cadence of prayer and the rapture of it all. He'd gather the fringes of his *tallit* and put his hands over his eyes as he said the *sh'ma,* the declaration of God's absolute oneness. He'd stand with his feet together for the *amidah,* the silent meditation. He taught me how to achieve that perfect balance necessary for proper *davening:* how to say every word clearly ("not mumbling"), but not loud enough to distract other worshipers nearby.

Sometimes it seemed that my father's greatest aspiration for me was to be the *shaliach tzibur,* the one who leads the prayers in the synagogue. Even before I reached my bar mitzvah, the age of majority that would magically make me eligible to lead the *davening,* my father practiced with me. He taught me *nusach,* the leader's special chant, and he explored with me ways to innovate within the traditional chant by adding contemporary Israeli and Hasidic songs, especially the music of Shlomo Carlebach. I remember walking to *shul* with him early in the morning, my hand in his, and not talking, but singing the songs of the synagogue through the sleepy streets.

As a teenager in the orbit of home and Jewish school, I

prayed daily, donning my *tefillin,* the leather straps and the leather boxes that contain handwritten biblical verses, six days a week (*tefillin* are not worn on the Sabbath or festivals). My daily worship became somewhat sporadic when I started to live on my own, and even into the early years of my marriage. The press of life seemed too overwhelming to take time for daily prayer. There was a job to get to and, later, children to rush off to school. Who had the time?

When my mother died, I reclaimed the daily prayer habit, and I attended synagogue whenever I could to say *kaddish.* But it didn't stick. When my year of *kaddish* was over, I stopped praying each day.

I again took on the habit of daily prayer two years later, this time not because of a family loss but because of a family gain. In 1997, my eldest child, Adam, had his bar mitzvah, and my father bought him a set of *tefillin.* As an adult Jewish male, he was expected to put them on for prayer each day. Could I do any less? I had to set an example, I thought, to show Adam that daily prayer with *tefillin* was a priority. In the years that followed, however, it was often Adam who reminded me of my daily prayer obligation.

And so by the time my father died I was, yet again, a consistent daily worshiper, although not a daily synagogue goer. My prayers were said at home. But returning to synagogue came naturally—as long as I could get out of bed in the mornings.

11

Even when I wasn't reciting the formal prayers each morning, I never lost the practice of saying the shorter Hebrew blessings, or *brachot,* on food or drink. The habit was reinforced in school and at the homes of both my parents. It became a habit that I liked. "*Baruch atah* Hashem . . ." "Blessed are you, Lord our God, Ruler of the universe, who brings forth bread from the earth." That was the one you said before eating any kind of bread. Sometimes it looked like we were talking to our food, but, in the end, it seemed right to give thanks. I was also careful about remembering to say the *Birchat Hamazon* (Grace After Meals), a short prayer of thanksgiving that was said when you finished eating a full meal. While most of the Hebrew prayers were formulaic, the grace had a section where you said a special blessing for assorted loved ones. As a kid I would say the parental add-on, "May the Merciful One bless my father and my mother and everyone seated here." As I grew older I added my wife, sons, and daughter to the prayer. Later I added my brothers, figuring they could use extra blessings too.

But then my mother died, and when we came from the

cemetery to my aunt and uncle's home for *shiva*, we all sat down for a solemn meal. Afterward, we said the grace, but when I got to the family blessing I stopped, feeling a bit confused. My mother was gone; how could I still bless her among the living? I had to think about how I was going to handle this.

One friend told me that he continues to bless his late father in the *Birchat Hamazon*, reasoning that the dead still need blessings. My feeling, however, was that for my blessing to have meaning for the living, my mother didn't belong among them. Four years later, when my father died, I deleted his name as well from the *Birchat Hamazon*. But where could I continue to acknowledge my mother and my father in my daily prayers?

My solution came in the first few weeks of mourning for my father. I was looking through the ArtScroll *siddur*, a heavily annotated prayer book, and found an unusual option. At the end of the silent *amidah* prayer, there was an insert that said: "Some recite verses pertaining to their names at this point."

A footnote at the bottom explained that "it is a source of merit to recite a Torah verse [at this point] that symbolizes one's name. . . . The verse should either contain the person's name or else begin and end with the first and last letters of his name. A list of such verses may be found on page 924."

I turned to page 924 and immediately spotted the biblical verse that matched my full Hebrew name, Aryeh. It is quite a famous verse, taken from Psalm 84. "Happy are those who dwell in your house; may they always praise you." Then I looked for the verse for my mother, whose Hebrew name was Yehudit. That verse also came from Psalms, from Number 146: "God protects and encourages the stranger, the orphan, and the widow, but the way of the wicked He contorts." And then I found the verse for my father, whose Hebrew name was Michael. "How goodly are your tents, O Jacob, your dwelling places, O Israel." That came from Chapter 24 in the Book of Numbers.

All three were verses quite well known to the daily worshiper. I decided that they would be the new acknowledgment of my parents in prayer. For the year of mourning for my father, I decided to forgo saying my own verse and say my parents' verses instead.

I mentioned this innovation to my uncle Norman and he improved on my plan. "Why don't you say your verse and then follow it with 'ben' (son of)—and then add your parents' verses?" This actually made a lot of sense. When you are referred to by name for Jewish ritual purposes—when you are called to the Torah reading in *shul* for an *aliyah,* when a prayer is said in *shul* for you if you're sick, when you are given your name by your parents as a newborn—it is your name plus "child of" your parent's name (father, mother, or both, depending on the situation and/or your religious custom). And so, once again, I had everyone taken care of. My living loved ones—my wife, children, and brothers—were blessed in the *Birchat Hamazon* and my mother and father were acknowledged by the mention of their verses in the daily morning prayer service. I inserted into my prayers my full name—Aryeh the son of Judith and Marvin—using the appropriate verse for each: "Happy are those who dwell in your house; may they always praise you," son of "God protects and encourages the stranger, the orphan, and the widow, but the way of the wicked He contorts," and of "How goodly are your tents, O Jacob, your dwelling places, O Israel."

While I may at times regret the absence of a more tangible inheritance and still harbor anger about their divorce, I know that I am the lucky child of generous parents. The riches they left me do not need to be probated in court. There is no estate tax. I am fortunate to have received a tradition of ritual practices, ethical principles, and sacred texts worth more than material possessions. Standing in the glow of my mother's Sabbath candelabra or wrapped in the warmth of my father's *tallit,* I am transported to another time and place. In a sense, I am with my parents and with the Divine.

Indeed, happy are those who dwell in your house.

12

There was only one woman who came to the weekday morning *minyan* at Ramath Orah with any regularity during the year I was saying *kaddish* for my father. On the morning of September 24, Lani* showed up at Ramath Orah and saw the note on the door announcing that the service had been moved to my home because of the death of my father. Lani, then a freshman at Columbia, made her way over to my apartment together with Dr. Schmeidler. As they walked, she mentioned to him that she was taking calculus. "He was telling me all these math jokes," she told me later. "I didn't really get them." I knew what she meant. As hard as I tried, I didn't get his jokes, either.

When they got to my apartment, a *minyan* was forming. Neither Lani nor my wife could be counted for an Orthodox *minyan,* but before long, we had the requisite ten men and the prayers commenced. Lani prayed in the dining room and the men gathered in the living room. After the *davening,* Lani asked if she could be of help, and Shira sent her down to the deli to get two containers of orange juice. "I was happy to help," Lani later told me. "I

---

* Not her real name, which she asked me not to use.

knew I couldn't count for a *minyan* so I was glad I could help in another way."

Lani got the juice but didn't hang around to drink any. She took off for Memorial Sloan-Kettering Cancer Center, where she regularly donated blood platelets. Lani also did volunteer tutoring of disadvantaged kids and, simply put, she struck me as one of the most selfless people on earth. Her mandate in life is to serve—both God and man—and she wants no recognition for any of it.

On most mornings, Lani attended the *minyan* at Columbia, which met at 8:00, an hour later than Ramath Orah's. A few times a week, however, she would come to our service so that she could get to an early class or to her Sloan-Kettering appointment. Going to daily *minyan* was part of Lani's life, even though, according to *halacha*, or traditional Jewish law, she was not required to do so to fulfill her obligation of daily prayer. (By most Orthodox interpretations, there is no requirement for women to say *kaddish* for a loved one who dies, although some rabbis allow them to do so, as long as they remain in the women's section of the synagogue.) Lani said that she was greatly influenced by the writings of Rabbi Joseph Soloveitchik of Yeshiva University on praying with a *minyan*. "When an individual prays on his or her own," Lani said, "the *tefillot* [prayers] go up [to heaven] on their own, but when you pray with a *minyan*, then the *tefillot* go up with all the merits of the *kahal* [congregation]. Why should I stand on my own two feet when I can go up with all these good people?" And, she noted, she can answer "amen" to the *kaddish* only at a *minyan*, as well as hear the Torah reading.

I asked her whether she felt frustrated that women were not counted in an Orthodox *minyan*. Her answer surprised me. She told me that she had "tremendous reverence" for *halacha*, and found no reason to question its wisdom in relieving women of the responsibility of participating in a *minyan*.

At this stage in her life, as a college student, voluntarily going to the daily *minyan* made sense, Lani said, but she hoped someday to marry and have children. Then, her first obligation will be not to the synagogue but to her family. "At this point, this is what I do best for my service of Hashem [God]," she said of going to *minyan*. "But when I'm a mother and my kid is crying, the best service of Hashem will be different."

Lani gave me some insight into Orthodox life at Columbia. In her classes, she and other Orthodox women competed with men for grades and recognition in class, but in the synagogue these same women accepted the rules that limited their participation. They sat behind the partition while the men led the service.

There were many daily prayer services at Columbia, not only in the morning, but in the afternoon and evening as well. In one of the dorms, there was a *minyan* for the evening service at eleven o'clock at night, held in a suite where Orthodox men lived. The women would gather in the suite's small kitchen. I didn't especially like going to these student services. I felt like I was intruding (who needed a professor around during off-hours?) and I was usually the only one saying *kaddish*. I could imagine them wondering, "who is that old man?"

13

Other women would come to our *minyan* only occasionally. One weekday morning in the fall a law student with a great head of wavy blond hair showed up, put on her own *tallit* and tefillin, and took a place on the women's side of the synagogue. When I got up to say *kaddish* she too rose and joined in. I wondered if she was a mourner. I introduced myself after the service, found out that her name was Ariela Migdal, and learned that she was saying *kaddish* for her grandfather at the request of her father, who was traveling to an academic conference in Germany and had asked Ariela to recite the *kaddish* he would not be able to say. "When he travels he asks different people to fill in for him," she explained.

Ariela grew up in a vibrant, egalitarian Conservative synagogue in Seattle. At her bat mitzvah, in the 1980s, for example, she read from the Torah and led the services. I was curious as to why she had chosen to come to Ramath Orah and stand on the other side of the a *mechitza,* when there were many Conservative synagogues in Manhattan where she could say *kaddish.* "I live across the street," she said, a bit apologetically. But she admitted to having a warm spot for the Orthodox service, even if it wasn't her first choice. "The grandfather I was saying *kaddish* for,

Benjamin Migdal, went to an Orthodox *shul* in Elizabeth, New Jersey. He was ninety-six when he died and for maybe the last thirty-five years, since he retired, he went to *minyan* every morning. He loved it. In some ways, this place reminds me of him," she said. I knew exactly what she meant. Ramath Orah reminded me of the *shul* I attended with my father. I felt closer to him when I was there.

14

Ariela and Lani were not the only ones in *shul* who could not be counted in the *minyan* when I first started saying *kaddish* at Ramath Orah. Chris Apap, the son of a church-going Catholic family in Michigan, came to Ramath Orah because he was dating a woman in the *shul* named Deb Kovsky. When I started saying *kaddish* in September, Chris was well on his way to converting to Judaism. He and Deb had gone to the same high school in the Detroit suburbs. He was an offensive guard on the football team and Deb was editor of the school paper. The first time they met, Deb interviewed Chris for an article she was writing and remembered him as a "cocky jock." A friendship grew but was interrupted when Chris went off to Wayne State University in Detroit and Deb to Harvard.

Deb moved to New York after college and Chris joined her. They both enrolled in Ph.D. programs, and because Judaism was a central part of Deb's life, Chris started to explore it, too. Together, he and Deb traveled to Israel for a visit. In Jerusalem, they attended a charismatic Friday night service, complete with Carlebach-style singing and dancing, at an unusual Orthodox synagogue called Yakar. They were still talking about Yakar when they returned to New York. A friend told them that if they liked Yakar, they'd love Ramath Orah. The couple was welcomed into our *shul*, and Chris began to study in earnest for his conversion.

Chris told me that the morning *minyan* was an important orientation to Judaism for him but that, prior to his conversion, not being counted when he came to *shul* was sometimes uncomfortable. "People would look around, see that there were ten men, but still couldn't start," he said. "I did cause some confusion." He said he did not feel bad about being excluded; he was learning that Judaism had its rules. But then came the conversion. On Friday morning, November 12, Chris went into the *mikveh*, the ritual bath, accompanied by an Orthodox *Beit Din*, or rabbinical court. He took the Hebrew name Yoni. After that, he became a member in good standing of our *minyan*. I asked him what it felt like. "I felt like I completed the community," he said. "It was something that really became quite wonderful for me."

15

It sometimes amazes me how well an Orthodox congregation can get along without a rabbi. With an educated laity—men who know how to lead the service and read the Torah—a congregation can run quite smoothly from morning to morning. In Judaism, the clergy are not intermediaries between mankind and the Divine the way they are in other faiths. There are no sacraments that only a rabbi can perform. A layman with skills can officiate at a wedding, funeral, bar mitzvah, or prayer service. Our part-time acting rabbi, Steven Friedman, was with us for two years before he was officially ordained. Just before I lost my father, Ramath Orah hired a bright young assistant rabbi, Yair Silverman. Like Rabbi Friedman, Yair was somewhat ambivalent about the rabbinate. He was not sure the pulpit was for him; Ramath Orah was something of a test. Also like Rabbi Friedman, he had a full-time job, as a management consultant for a firm in Midtown.

One of Yair's responsibilities at Ramath Orah was overseeing the daily *minyan*. While the order of the service is set, Yair did his best to knit together the disparate *minyan* members into a community. At the end of the service he'd conduct a brief class in Jewish law, and then make a few synagogue-related announcements, acknowledging a visitor, a *yahrtzeit,* a birthday, or some other event in the life of the congregation. Although he had a job to run off to, he would stay for a few minutes after the service to answer a question or make a suggestion. I often turned to him for advice on *kaddish* and mourning rituals. And in the process, I learned a little about him. Before he went off to Yeshiva University's rabbinical school, Yair lived in Israel and served in the Israeli army. In Israel, hitchhiking is an essential form of transportation for soldiers, and he once got a ride from a town near the Lebanese border all the way to Jerusalem. During the two-hour drive, he found out that the driver, a man in his seventies, was a secular kibbutznik who claimed to have no religious life except for one thing: every year he would say *kaddish* for his brother. Both he and his brother were refugees from Hitler's Europe who came to Israel in the early 1940s. Yair could not remember the driver's name, but he remembered the name of the brother, Mordecai, and that he was a soldier who fell on Independence Day, May 5, 1948. "I've said *kaddish* for him all these years," the driver said. "But who will say it when I'm gone? Would you please carry on for me? Say *kaddish* for Mordecai."

"I've tried to honor that," Yair told me. Every year on Israeli Independence Day, Yair says *kaddish* to honor this soldier he never knew.

Just about everyone, I was discovering, had a *kaddish* story.

Winter

1

Never mind the calendar. In our family, winter in New York begins on Thanksgiving Day. Although it may eventually clear up, the day inevitably starts out windy and cold. We get up early and search through the bottom of the front hallway dresser, looking for last winter's hats and gloves. It's been our tradition for the last several years to watch the Macy's Thanksgiving Day Parade from the home of our friends, Sam Schacter and Evelyn Musher. They've got a great apartment on Central Park West, where dozens of their friends gather for the occasion. The huge parade balloons—Garfield and Bullwinkle and Spider-Man among them—float right past their windows. The trick is to get to the apartment early, around 9:00 A.M., before the parade steps off a few blocks away at the Museum of Natural History.

On secular holidays like Thanksgiving, when worshipers don't have to rush off to work, synagogues like Ramath Orah start the morning *minyan* an hour later, in our case at 8:00 A.M. I didn't want to arrive late for the parade, so I sought out an earlier *minyan*. A friend told me about the small Hasidic synagogue he goes to on Ninety-first street, known simply as Rabbi Vorhand's *shul*. They apparently don't give a hoot about secular holidays like Thanksgiving. Their *minyan* starts at 7:00 A.M.

I said *kaddish* at Rabbi Vorhand's *shul* and then linked up with Shira and the kids, who were on their way to Sam and Evelyn's. Adam, Emma, and Judah gawked out the window while we enjoyed brunch and greeted friends, many of whom we hadn't seen in a year. I mentioned to Sam that Thanksgiving at his house was such a tradition for my family that I even caught an early *minyan* to get there on time. "I'm an *avel,*" I added, using the Hebrew word for mourner, feeling somehow that I had to explain all this *minyan*-going.

Sam reprimanded me. "Never apologize for going to *minyan.* There's nothing to explain." He added: "For thirty years, I go every morning. You don't have to be an *avel* to go to daily *minyan.*"

Yes, I said, I'd like to be a regular at the morning *minyan,* but the job and the school bus and packing lunches— He cut me off. "You're working it out now?" he asked without waiting for an answer. "You can always work out going to *minyan.*"

A friend—another daily *minyan*-goer—joined the conversation and told a macabre *shul* joke. Two rabbis met in the park and began to talk about the struggle to get the ten men needed for the morning *minyan.* "*Baruch* Hashem [Thank God]," one of them said, "we just had a member die and leave four sons. Four sons! We're set for the year."

Of course, morning *minyan* is for more than mourners. In my *shul*, there wouldn't be a *minyan* for the mourners to say *kaddish* if there weren't others who felt it was important to come each morning. Still, Sam's admonition made me think about why I was so quick to explain what I was doing each morning in *shul*. Was it that I did not want to appear overly pious? Was I looking for sympathy? A little of both, I suspect.

Later that day we drove out to Great Neck, Long Island, to join Shira's family for Thanksgiving dinner at the home of her brother Mordi. I was eager to get to Great Neck early so I could catch the afternoon *mincha* service at the local synagogue before the family dinner. Shira dropped me off at the Young Israel of Great Neck, a synagogue just a few blocks from Mordi's house, and I joined the service and said *kaddish* with the other mourners. Afterward, one of the synagogue regulars came over to greet me. He looked awfully familiar, and when he introduced himself as Michael Frank, I immediately remembered him as a college classmate. We exchanged a few pleasantries and then he asked: "What brings you here?"

I was about to explain that I was an *avel* and needed to say *kaddish*. But I stopped myself, smiled, and said: "I'm in the neighborhood for Thanksgiving and thought I'd catch *mincha*."

2

I was especially zealous that Thanksgiving weekend about catching every service—morning, afternoon, and evening—because I was operating without my "*kaddish* safety net." The requirement in Jewish law is for at least one family member, preferably a child of the deceased, to say *kaddish* at each of the three daily services. Since I have two brothers, and Dov could be depended on to say *kaddish* three times a day almost without fail, I didn't feel terrible if I occasionally missed a service. At least Dov was saying *kaddish*, I reasoned. Dov was my safety net. Prior to the Thanksgiving weekend, however, Dov called to tell me that he'd be traveling to visit friends in Florida. In all likelihood, he would not be near a synagogue. The responsibility for saying *kaddish* fell squarely on my shoulders.

In the first few weeks after my father died, I was especially careful about *kaddish*. I went to Ramath Orah every morning and usually caught one of the many afternoon and evening student-run prayer services at Columbia.

But as the winter approached, I began to slacken off. After Thanksgiving, with the days getting shorter and colder, I decided to leave the afternoon and evening services to Dov. I concentrated on getting to the morning *minyan* at Ramath Orah. Since I was the only actual *avel,* I was also in the *chiyuv* category, which meant that I led the service every morning. It was something I enjoyed doing occasionally—it was one of the things my dad had taught me, and I know that he was pleased that I was good at it— but it meant that I had to stand throughout the service and recite many of the prayers out loud. Aside from the physical demands, the spiritual responsibility of leading everyone else in prayer was starting to get to me.

It was around this time that I ran into Rabbi Avi Weiss, a modern Orthodox rabbi from Riverdale, New York, who is well known for his political activism but less so for his excellent pastoral skills. Rabbi Weiss had visited me four years earlier, when I was sitting *shiva* for my mother, and I found his visit to be one of the most comforting. He asked me how *kaddish* for my father was going. "Fine," I told him. "But I'm getting tired of being *shaliach tzibur.* I do it every day and it's just wearing me out."

Rabbi Weiss told me that the same thing happened to him after his mother died. He found that leading the service every day was exhausting and so he stopped. He still came to *shul* each morning, but he was not the *shaliach tzibur.* Rabbi Weiss explained that the term *chiyuv,* which literally means "obligation," does not mean that the mourner is required to lead the service. The real obligation is to remember the departed. For some, that means being the *shaliach tzibur;* for others, it means saying *kaddish.* Although the rabbi didn't say it, I imagine for still others it might mean studying a sacred text, or reading Auden, or listening to Mahler. Each of us has to remember in the way that is best for us. For me, saying *kaddish* daily worked.

3

The daily *minyan* at Ramath Orah began to thin out in December. From the time I started saying *kaddish* in late September, we had a *minyan* every morning. While I had missed some afternoon and evening services, I had a perfect attendance record in the morning. I hadn't missed a day of saying at least one *kaddish* since my father died. The *shul* had a solid core of ten daily worshipers and a handful of others. Most mornings we'd have fourteen or fifteen. But Monday, December 13—I remember the date because I recorded it in my diary—I could barely get out of bed. I had been up late the night before and my throat was sore. I dragged myself to *shul* through a freezing morning rain and got there ten minutes late. I was the eighth man. We waited. It was 7:15. We looked out the door, although we didn't know who we were looking for. Who could possibly pass by that would be willing to join us? We went to the phones. All we got were answering machines. People obviously didn't want to be bothered. Finally, we reached a Columbia senior, Ben Strauss, who lived a couple of blocks away and would often help with the *minyan* if we were in a pinch. He said he'd come right over. By 7:30, we had only nine and were about to give up. But then our tenth man lumbered around the corner and into *shul*. We made it. I went to the *bimah* and began to lead the prayers. My throat hurt, but it felt good.

In the days that followed, we had many more close calls. We hit rock bottom on the morning of December 30. When I arrived at 7:00, we were six. By 7:15, we were seven. We went to the phones, but no one was answering. All the Columbia students were away for the semester break. At 7:20, we were eight. And then no one else came. We prayed in the synagogue, but by ourselves, without a *minyan*. I did not say *kaddish*. I thought of trying to find another *minyan* at another *shul*, but I needed to get home. Shira was on a business trip, and the kids were alone, waiting for me. It was the first day since my father died that I did not say *kaddish*, and I realized that more would follow. On another morning it would be something else, perhaps a class or a flight to catch. I suppose I could have found a more dependable *minyan*, but my bond with my *shul* was strong. The men there were depending on me as much as I was depending on them. And besides, it was in Ramath Orah, more than in any other *shul*, that I sensed my parents' presence. That was where my mourning had its greatest resonance, whether I was able to say *kaddish* or not. I decided to set a new standard for my *kaddish* routine. Every day I would *try* to say *kaddish*. I would go to Ramath Orah in the hope of finding a *minyan*, but if we didn't get one, I would feel as though I had done my best and let it go.

4

One Monday in December there were only ten worshipers in *shul,* which meant that during the Torah reading, half of us were standing at the table on which the scroll was laid out. One of the sextons that morning was Philip Sandberg, a hearty ninety-year-old Polish Holocaust survivor, who came to *shul* every morning. I received an *aliyah,* so I stood next to Mr. Sandberg, who always remembered to say a prayer for his ailing wife, Pauline, before the open Torah. "Pescha bas Devorah," he would cry out, using her Hebrew name. The Torah reader was about to begin when Mr. Sandberg began to shake violently. His hands, his head, his upper torso seemed seized by an outside force. His eyes suddenly rolled back in his head, his legs buckled, and he came crashing down, his face on the open Torah scroll. Then he lifted his head, stood up, and began shaking again. Finally, his feet gave way and he fell to the floor.

We immediately stopped the service. Two of us lifted Mr. Sandberg, and a third brought a chair for him to sit on. I took his hand; it was ice cold. I began to slap his forearm. His eyes were closed and he was unresponsive. We quickly removed his *tallit* and *tefillin* and wiped his forehead. It too was cold and clammy.

Ben Strauss pulled the cell phone off his belt and called

Hatzolah, the reliable Jewish volunteer ambulance service. Hatzolah knew the location of every synagogue in town and had a much better response time than the hospital ambulances.

We were doing everything we could to stimulate Mr. Sandberg, talking to him and gently slapping his arms and his face. Someone brought a glass of water but he would not drink. "Don't die," I whispered. I was sure he was dying. It was bad enough that I wasn't at my father's side when he died, I thought, but now I am a witness to the death of another man whose son was not at his side.

Within minutes, the Hatzolah paramedics were coming through the front door. They gave Mr. Sandberg some smelling salts and he came to. As they carried him out on a stretcher, he turned to me and said in Yiddish, "Get my *tallis* and *tefillin*."

The Hatzolah ambulance took Mr. Sandberg to St. Luke's Hospital, which is three blocks from the *shul*. I called that night and was told that he was admitted for "monitoring" overnight. I later learned that he was suffering from dehydration and an ulcer attack. A few days later, he was back in *shul*.

Both of Mr. Sandberg's sons live in Manhattan, and eleven years earlier they had moved their parents from their Bronx home to an apartment in a building they owned on 110th Street, so that they would be better able to look after them. But Mrs. Sandberg became ill shortly after the move, and had to be put into a nearby nursing home. Mr. Sandberg spent most of his day with her, but his son Lou told me that he was also developing a tendency to wander off. One time he wound up on the East Side, disoriented and dehydrated, and was picked up by an ambulance and taken to the hospital. Lou and his brother worry about their father. They come by his apartment every day to set out his clothes and take him to the barber for a shave, and they stop by often during the day to see if he's okay.

I've heard similar stories from other friends with aging parents. When Lou finished telling me his story I said something that, in retrospect, seemed a bit bold and brash. Certainly not my usual diplomatic self. I guess I was speaking part in sympathy and part in jealousy. I looked at him and said: "I'm sure it's a great burden having ailing parents who need so much care, but—I'll tell you from experience—what you're doing is a whole lot better than saying *kaddish*."

Lou seemed to take it the right way. "I hear you," he said. "I hear you."

5

"God always provides mourners" goes an old Yiddish expression. With Mr. Sandberg temporarily on the bench, a new regular worshiper suddenly materialized in *shul*. Melvin's* mother died on December 3, just ten weeks after my father died. He came quietly into *shul* one day in mid-December, sat in the last row, and prayed silently. When it came time for me to say *kaddish,* I heard him saying it along with me. After services, we traded stories of disease and loss. He told me that his mother died of aplastic anemia. "Do you know what that is?" he asked. I didn't really want to know, but he seemed to want to tell me. She died a few days after she became sick, he said. My father also died quickly, I told him. Heart attack.

Melvin, who was roughly my age, then told me about his religious journey. When he was a child, Melvin's family attended an Orthodox *shul,* kept kosher, and was generally observant, with one caveat: after services on Saturday morning, his father would open the family business—a shoe store in downtown Scranton. When Melvin was in third grade, he pointed out the inconsistency and con-

* Not his real name, which he asked me not to use.

vinced his father to keep the store closed on the Sabbath. The family then became fully observant, and Melvin made sure that everyone towed the line.

After graduating college, however, Melvin began having doubts about his religious beliefs. He eventually stopped going to synagogue and stopped observing the Sabbath. His father took it in stride, but his mother, he recalled, "was heartbroken."

With her death, Melvin came back to the synagogue to mourn for her properly. He knew it was something she would have wanted him to do. "She was a very pious woman," Melvin said.

I was sorry for Melvin's loss, but I was happy to have his company. I was no longer the only mourner in the congregation. There's nothing worse than saying *kaddish* alone in *shul*. You feel self-conscious and singled out in a way that gives new meaning to the term *Kaddish Yatom, Mourner's Kaddish*. When you say *kaddish* alone, you feel especially orphaned.

6

Chanukah came early that year. The first day fell on December 8 rather than at the end of the month, nearer to Christmas, the way it usually does. The day before the holiday, an envelope arrived from Teme. "Wishing you and the children a Happy Chanukah," she wrote. Inside were three generous checks, one for each of the kids. "Tell the children to buy something special for the holiday. Love, Teme."

Cards and gifts continued to arrive for each holiday and each child's birthday. I was overwhelmed by her thoughtfulness and, in a small way, felt that my father was still remembering us.

Chanukah also brought my friend Elie Spitz, to New York. Elie, a rabbi whose sabbatical in Israel coincided with the one I took with my family in 1997–1998, is the rabbi of a Conservative congregation in Tustin, California, outside Los Angeles. As a congregational rabbi, he has had a host of experiences with death and bereavement. Through his work and personal experiences, he came to embrace the traditional belief in the Jewish afterlife and even wrote a book about it, *Does the Soul Survive: A Jewish Journey to Belief in the Afterlife, Past Lives, and Living with Purpose.* I had always approached the subject of the afterlife with some uncertainty, but the loss of my mother and father made me realize that they were not gone but in a real sense still with me.

Elie had been something of a long-distance grief counselor to me since my father's death and I looked forward to his visit. I had mentioned to Elie that our morning *minyan* was on shaky ground. "What time do you *daven*?" he asked on the eve of his visit.

"Seven A.M., but I don't want you to come," I responded. "Elie, that's 4:00 A.M. for you. Don't knock yourself out."

But a couple of days later, Elie was in *shul*. He had arrived in New York from Los Angeles the night before and got to Ramath Orah even earlier than I did. "Thanks, but you didn't have to come," I told him.

"I came because I really wanted to answer 'amen' to your *kaddish*," he replied.

7

Chanukah also meant that 1999 was drawing to a close. The whole world seemed giddy with millennial fever. Millennial countdown clocks were on sale at the drugstore for those who wanted to know exactly how many hours, minutes, and seconds were left to the big day. No one knew exactly what to expect. There was endless talk about Y2K bugs in our computers and the threat of terrorist attacks at New Year's Eve celebrations.

It was also an exciting time for me professionally. I was in my sixth year of teaching as an assistant professor at Columbia, and I would soon be up for tenure. In the academic system, either you get tenure after seven years or you have to leave the university. I very much wanted to stay. For one thing, I had given up a tenured job at the *New York Times* to teach. And I discovered that I loved teaching, was succeeding at it, and wanted very much to continue doing it. I was a bit unsure of myself in the classroom at first, but with time my confidence grew. I had always considered myself a natural writer, but never a natural teacher. Writing for a million people—as I did daily at the *Times*—never fazed me, but I used to dread speaking in public. My readers were nameless and faceless; my students were real people. If I made a mistake at the computer, there was always the delete button; if I said the wrong thing to a class, there was no taking it back.

As the old saying goes, my students taught me how to teach. I learned as much from them as I did from my own teachers and colleagues. I found that I had an ability to explain what I did as a writer and reporter. And my students had learned the lessons, graduated, and were working at some of the top newspapers in the country, including the *Times,* the *Daily News,* the *Washington Post,* the *Hartford Courant,* the *Baltimore Sun,* and the *Detroit Free Press.*

I was meeting with success in another realm, too— raising money for the university. Joan Konner, the dean who had hired me at Columbia, believed that the school could get foundations to support individual courses. She thought my spring seminar, Covering Religion, should be able to attract foundation support. Joan and I shopped the idea to several foundations, and one of them, Scripps Howard, bought it. The Scripps Howard Foundation is the philanthropic arm of the E. W. Scripps Company, a huge national media chain that has a special interest in journalism education. Scripps established a religion program at the Journalism School and made me its director. In its first few years, the program organized conferences in religion and journalism. But then I proposed something more ambitious. I suggested using the grant to take the students in my Covering Religion class to Israel. I argued that such a trip was essential if our students were to fully understand the three great Abrahamic faiths—Judaism, Christianity, and Islam. This was the trip I was planning when I traveled to Israel back in August, when I spent my last days with my father.

Although raising money was certainly valued at the university, it wasn't enough to guarantee my being awarded tenure. More important than money—and even more important than teaching skills—are publications. They are said to be the ultimate test of a scholar's mettle. My first book, *The Search for God at Harvard,* had been published in 1991. And I had a second one in the works as well, which was scheduled to be published just as I was entering my all-important seventh year.

The prospect of my new book, *Being Jewish: The Spiritual and Cultural Practice of Judaism Today,* also made for some excitement. By December, most of the writing and editing had been completed, and I was very pleased with the interior design and with the cover. One thing that still needed to be decided on was the dedication page. Since the book was about Jewish ritual, I thought the most appropriate dedication would be to my parents, who were my first and best teachers of Judaism. But I struggled with the wording. Children of divorce don't really have "parents." I never felt that I did. I had a mother and a father, but that was it. I never spoke about going to "my parents' home" the way other kids did. I never said I was going to see "my parents." I couldn't borrow my "parents' car" or spend a vacation with "my parents." "Parents" just wasn't part of my vocabulary. But perhaps, as Emma had suggested, I was no longer the child of divorce. If so, were they now, once again, my parents? Still, it didn't sit right. I decided to dedicate the book "To the memory of my mother and my father." I thought it was an appropriate way to honor them.

I mentioned the dedication to my stepparents via e-mail, thinking that they would be pleased that I was honoring their spouses.

Teme sent back an e-mail from Jerusalem saying that she thought the dedication was just right. My mother and father deserved to be recognized, especially in a book about Jewish ritual, she wrote. Jack, however, was not at all pleased. He didn't feel that it was appropriate to mention them together on the same page, and we argued about it for a while. I couldn't change his mind, and when *Being Jewish* was published, with the dedication as I had planned it, he was angry. Divorce, I was beginning to discover, is one of those things that survives even death. Divorce is for all eternity.

8

Even before she married Jack, my mother had a taste for the finer things. She'd buy only the best kosher cuts of meat and fresh breads, fish, and vegetables. Canned or frozen foods were not her thing. As a single mother, she couldn't afford personal luxuries, but sometimes she would indulge herself. She was always handsomely dressed and never in synthetics; in the Dacron polyester 1960s, she wore cottons and wools. She was a voracious reader, a true lover of literature, who hated paperbacks; she read only clothbound books. (Luckily she was a high school librarian, so she could get almost any title she wanted for free—and in hardcover.) Most of all, she had a love for classical music. She bought records and went to the symphony or opera whenever she could. She would drop everything to see Leonard Bernstein conduct. I remember one winter Saturday when I was fourteen years old. She was reading the *Times* arts page and saw that Bernstein was conducting that night at Lincoln Center. Beethoven's Ninth was on the program. "Let's go," she said.

"Mom, I'm sure it's sold out," I said.

"I'm sure it is," she said, "but let's go anyway."

As soon as the Sabbath was over, we rushed down to

Lincoln Center. Sure enough, the box office had a big SOLD OUT sign on the window. My mother spotted a small crowd around a man holding two tickets. There was a negotiation going on. Mom plowed into the crowd, grabbed the tickets, and thrust $20 into his hands. This was in 1964, when the best Philharmonic seats went for $4.50. Twenty dollars was our food budget for the week. (No steaks that week.) But Mom couldn't be happier. We sat in the orchestra.

My mother married Jack in 1970, and our lives began to change. He was a corporate executive, and we enjoyed the perks. We flew to the Caribbean on the corporate jet. We stayed at fancy hotels. We had a country house and a city apartment. Mom was Cinderella and we, her sons, were the mice who were suddenly transformed into handsome steeds. We benefited from being in her orbit.

Years later, when Shira first met my mother, she sized her up this way: "Your mother is someone who knows that luxuries are sometimes necessities." In the early years of our marriage, as Shira and I struggled with the necessities, my mother showered us with the extras. She took us to the theater, the ballet, the opera. She'd bestow Broadway tickets on us and take the children to *The Nutcracker*. When Adam developed an interest in Mozart, she took him to a performance of *Don Giovanni* at the Met. We paid our own grocery bill, of course, but for years my mother picked up our bill at the kosher butcher (first cuts only). We paid our children's considerable day-school tuition, but she picked up the cost of their music and ballet lessons. She took us (and later our children) shopping at stores we would never go into, like Saks and Bloomingdale's.

In the year after my mother's death, I didn't want luxuries. Following Jewish mourning practices, I didn't listen to music for the year and I didn't buy new clothes. I was coming to terms with losing one of the greatest necessities of life: a loving mother. Mine was gone and I was in mourning.

Two years after my mother's death, I got a call from a teaching colleague at Columbia, Elizabeth Dribben, asking if I was interested in tickets to *Phantom of the Opera* on Broadway. Liz, an adjunct professor who taught radio, was a longtime New York radio producer and personality, and was on some of the best press lists in the city. She began to fill the gap in our family's theater-going life that resulted from my mother's death. We referred to her as our "cultural fairy-godmother."

When Liz called with an offer of tickets after Dad died, I explained that since I was in mourning, I was taking a break from the theater. I sent the other members of my family instead. Adam, Emma, and Shira reaped the benefits. But when Liz called in mid-December with an offer to hear Handel's *Messiah* sung by a gospel group at Avery

Fisher Hall, I couldn't resist. While mourning for my father, I hadn't been as careful about not listening to music as I'd been when I was mourning for my mother; my main expression of mourning for my father was, I felt, through saying *kaddish* in the synagogue. I decided to go.

Handel's *Messiah* occupies a special place in my life. It represented one of my first stabs at independence and a branching out beyond my parochial Jewish world. I had never heard of the *Messiah* until I was seventeen years old and living with my father in Hartford. It was my senior year in high school, and although I had lived with my mother since I was in first grade, I decided to spend this year with my father. The reason was a rather practical one: I was not doing well in the *yeshiva* high school I was attending in Brooklyn. My grades were suffering because of the dual curriculum of Hebrew and English. I thought that a year at a public school would offer me the boost that I needed to get into college. I decided to live with my father for my senior year and attend the local public school, Weaver High. My father, who was then living with his parents in Hartford, seemed to enjoy having me with him. He saw my year in public school as a temporary solution to a problem. He expected me to follow in his footsteps and attend Yeshiva University in New York, which I did.

Weaver had an excellent music program. It was there

that I first heard the *Messiah*. I already knew about operas and symphonies, but the *Messiah* was my first oratorio. I liked the notion of a beautiful and intricate fully orchestrated four-part religious song of praise. It wasn't like anything I had ever heard in a synagogue.

The next year, when I was back in New York as a freshman at Yeshiva University, I saw in the *Times* that the *Messiah* was playing at Carnegie Hall. I went downtown to the box office and bought two tickets, hoping to bring a date. But I was a terribly shy college freshman and couldn't muster the courage to ask a girl to accompany me. I asked friends at school, but no one wanted to go. The whole thing sounded terribly *goyish,* they said. Even my roommate wouldn't go. I ended up heading down to Carnegie Hall myself, selling my extra ticket and sitting somewhat uneasily through the performance. Was I really supposed to be there as the choir sang "For unto us a child is born"? Was I really supposed to stand for the Hallelujah chorus? When I got back to the dorm, a surprise awaited me. As a joke, my roommate and some other friends had taken books off my shelf and made an enormous cross on the floor. At the top, they put the score of the *Messiah.*

I'm not sure why, some thirty years later, in the year of mourning for my father, I felt compelled to go again. Maybe it reminded me of the year I spent with him. Maybe it was just an opportunity I didn't want to pass up. It was an unusual performance. Handel's wonderful music was sung to an enthusiastic gospel beat by a hand-clapping, foot-stomping choir of 100 voices. I enjoyed it, but as I had thirty years before, I sat somewhat uneasily through the performance. Was I really supposed to be there?

It wasn't the last time that I went to hear music during the year of mourning for my father. A few weeks after the *Messiah*, I attended a Broadway show and later a bar mitzvah party with a live band. I went and even enjoyed myself, but I felt a heaviness in my heart. The music didn't lift my soul the way it always did. Something weighed heavily on me. Maybe, I thought, there was wisdom in the tradition that mourners should abstain from music.

9

For millions around the world, the new year hasn't officially arrived until the ball drops in New York's Times Square. However, the timing for the millennial New Year's Eve of 1999 wasn't great for observant Jews. As it fell on a Friday night, we couldn't fully participate in the festivities—travel to parties or to the fireworks in Central Park. We couldn't even watch it on television, or blow a horn at midnight.

A debate ensued among traditional rabbis about what to do. Some rabbis argued that it would be appropriate to hold special Sabbath celebrations at local synagogues so that observant Jews could usher in the second millennium together. Instead of red wine on Friday night, we could drink Champagne. Other rabbis were dead set against it. The Sabbath had a sanctity that overrode any secular celebration. The New Year's date, marking the first year in the life of Jesus, was not an occasion for Jewish celebration. This should be a Sabbath like any other Sabbath, they said.

Happily, we belong to two synagogues that took the former approach. We spent the first part of New Year's Eve at Ramath Orah, where we had a traditional Sabbath dinner after the services. Shabbat dinners at Ramath Orah have a particularly homey feeling to them. The congregation orders food from a local kosher caterer but doesn't hire waiters or kitchen staff; we dish out and serve the food ourselves. The dinner preparations were taking a bit longer than usual that night and my four-year-old son, Judah, was complaining of hunger. I took him by the hand and led him into the kitchen. The table there was laden with Shabbat specialties of *challah,* roast chicken, meatballs, salads, and potato concoctions. Around the table were half a dozen women with smiling faces, ready to accommodate a preschooler's rush of hunger.

Suddenly I felt like I was four years old and holding my father's hand in some Sabbath kitchen of my childhood. My nose barely came up to the top of the table. It all felt so comforting. Someone handed Judah a plate with some chicken and we were off. But my spell was not broken.

Later that evening, after the Ramath Orah dinner, we walked the ten blocks to Shira's preferred synagogue, Ansche Chesed, for Champagne, a cappella singing, and a skit on the lighter side of 1,000 years of Jewish history. There were party hats and noisemakers, and special activities aimed at keeping little kids awake beyond their bedtimes. We counted down the seconds as 2000 approached and, at the stroke of midnight, wished each other a "Happy New Year" and a *"Gut Shabbos."* As we made our way home after midnight, hundreds of holiday celebrants in party hats and tuxedos were on the Manhattan streets. We were happy that we had both kept the Sabbath and were part of a great moment in secular history.

I was with my wife and children that night, but in a private sense I felt alone. I was acutely aware that I was going into the new millennium without my parents to hold on to. I wanted them there. I wanted them to experience this extraordinary passage. I wanted my mother there to tell me that it was all right, that I had nothing to fear from the twenty-first century. Why wasn't my father there telling me that this was just a moment in history, that we Jews could weather this as we had the last 4,000 years. He could put it all in perspective. I was angry. Where were my parents?

Two weeks later, on January 15, the *New York Times* ran a fascinating front-page article that suggested that hundreds of New Yorkers actually "willed themselves to live" into the new millennium. Figures from the New York City Health Department showed that 1,791 people died in the first week of 2000, 604 more than died in the same period a year earlier, an increase of 50.8 percent. Richard M. Suzman of the National Institute on Aging, explained: "It's pretty well established that people who are seriously ill will hang on to reach significant events, whether it be birthdays, anniversaries, or religious holidays. In this case, making it into the next century or millennium counts as that."

"The will to live can be pretty powerful," added Robert N. Butler, founder and president of the International Longevity Center.

Why didn't my parents will themselves to live, just a few more months or years into the new millennium? I wish they had. Both for them and for me.

10

On Saturday, January 1, 2000, there was a robust—if slightly hung over—*minyan* at Ramath Orah. Nearly a hundred people attended. Some had been up late the night before celebrating, but they also wanted to start the year right—in synagogue. The next day, Sunday, I counted sixteen worshipers. But on Monday, an unseasonably warm and sunny day, we had only seven.

When I arrived at *shul* that morning, I noticed that a homeless man had taken up residence on the front stoop. It was a situation that we had unfortunately grown accustomed—and even callous—to. New York City was full of homeless men and women who chose not to go to a public shelter but to sleep on the streets instead. Many were mentally ill. Usually they occupied some stoop for a day or two and then moved on.

Since there was no *minyan* that morning, I was unable to say *kaddish,* but I felt that I gave it my best shot. On Tuesday, the homeless man was there again when I arrived at *shul.* Inside, we waited for a *minyan,* but only eight men came.

Rabbi Silverman, Ramath Orah's assistant rabbi, finally suggested a connection. "Maybe we're getting a message from on high about the man on our stoop," he said.

"Maybe what's going on outside is more important than what's going on in here."

I left *shul* and approached the homeless man. He lay across the upper step, in front of a set of double doors that are usually closed. On the two lower steps were a ragged pair of leather shoes and an array of garbage—take-out containers, coffee cups, and crumpled aluminum foil. Parked on the sidewalk was a shopping cart laden with plastic bags that seemed stuffed with old clothes and rags. The man reeked.

Swaddled in stained blankets, he roused when I approached. The area over his left eye was cut and swollen. "Can I get you a cup of coffee?" I asked. "Two sugars," he responded. "And a ham and cheese sandwich."

Unaccustomed as I am to buying ham and cheese, I went to the delicatessen around the corner and returned with the sandwich. The man was asleep so I just left the food on the step for him and went home.

Later that day, I called the New York City Coalition for the Homeless. The clerk who answered the phone recommended that I send the man to their offices at 89 Chambers Street; they'd refer him to a shelter. I said that I had a feeling that the man wouldn't want to go. He seemed quite comfortable on our stoop. I asked the clerk if he could send a caseworker to our synagogue to talk to the man and encourage him to take advantage of the shelter system.

"I'm afraid that's impossible," the clerk said. "We're understaffed right now."

"What should we do?" I asked. "Just let him stay out there? It's cold. He could freeze to death."

"Well, if he's a nuisance, you can always call the police."

That might have been a solution, but it didn't seem like what this was all about.

On Wednesday, the homeless man was there outside the *shul* again. Inside, we again failed to get a *minyan*—for the third day in a row. Afterward, I told the man about the coalition offices and urged him to go. "I've been at those shelters," he told me. "All they do is rip you off there. I got jumped there and stabbed in the eye," he said, pointing to his injury.

"Well, you've got to find a warm place," I said, "you're going to freeze here."

The man did not respond. I handed him a piece of paper with the address and phone number of the Coalition for the Homeless.

He was on the stoop again on Thursday. Quite remarkably, that day our *minyan* revived. We had eleven.

A few days later the homeless man was gone.

11

You could tell it was Monday or Thursday morning at Ramath Orah if Professor Louis Henkin was there. Mondays and Thursdays, the days on which the Torah is read, were the weekday mornings Professor Henkin set aside for synagogue attendance. He was passionate about the necessity for a *shul* to have a daily *minyan*. "A *shul* without a daily *minyan* is not a *shul*," Professor Henkin once told me.

He didn't like it when I would call him Professor Henkin. "Call me Lou," he said when I joined the Columbia faculty. When I politely said yes but continued to call him Professor Henkin, he began to call me "Professor Goldman." He wouldn't call me Ari until I called him Lou. It wasn't easy. I was merely an assistant professor. He was a University Professor, a title bestowed on just a handful of distinguished Columbia faculty. There are only four University Professors at Columbia at any one time. While most professors can teach only within their discipline, University Professors can teach anything, university-wide. When I first met him, Professor Henkin had been on the faculty of the Law School for nearly forty years. He was one of the professors who had created the specialty of human rights law. In his honor, the Law School established the Louis Henkin Professorship in Human Rights. In the 1940s, as a young Harvard-trained lawyer, he had clerked for two of the most outstanding jurists of the twentieth century, Federal Court of Appeals Judge Learned Hand, and United States Supreme Court Justice Felix Frankfurter. How could I call him Lou?

Professor Henkin, who was born in Russia in 1917 and was brought to America as a child, was the son of a renowned author and scholar, Rabbi Yosef Eliyahu Henkin, whose annotated Jewish calendar, the *Ezras Torah Luach,* is still the standard in most Orthodox synagogues. For nearly fifty years, Rabbi Henkin was the head of an Orthodox relief organization known as Ezras Torah, which provides assistance to poor Jews around the world and was especially active in rescue efforts during and after the Holocaust. In his beard and long coat, he was a familiar figure on the national scene, lobbying for European Jewry.

Professor Henkin—tall, lanky, and clean-shaven—was more than just personally committed to the *minyan* at Ramath Orah; he also believed others must do their part. "You have to see attendance at the *minyan* as a communal obligation," he said. "It is part of what it means to be a member of a congregation."

He told me that he drew inspiration from a man he got to know when he lived in Washington in the 1950s. He remembered the man as "Mr. Brooks" and said that he was someone who came to *shul* daily to help make the *minyan.* "Mr. Brooks used to say, 'We've carried this on our backs for two thousand years. We can't drop it now.' "

I wondered out loud why he cited Mr. Brooks and not his own father, Rabbi Henkin. Didn't your father instill an ethic of daily *minyan* attendance in you? I asked.

"No. He took all these things for granted. He believed that I *davened* every day and he was right. I continued to put on *tefillin* during four years of army service—most of it in combat—almost without a break."

Four years in the army? I asked.

"Four years, one month, and twenty days. I was an artillery observer."

I was impressed—both about the *tefillin* and the combat service.

Professor Henkin may not be conspicuous about his Judaism, but it is rock solid. "I come from a time and maybe a place where one wore one's Judaism unobtrusively. I am not here [at Columbia] as a Jewish professor. I am a professor who is a Jew." Professor Henkin's views struck a responsive chord within me, and I asked him one day about his experience of saying *kaddish.* He told me two fascinating stories.

One day during his clerkship for Frankfurter he found the judge in a pensive mood, thinking about his death. He told the young Henkin: "You know I'm not religious, but I was born a Jew and I want the world to know that I was a Jew. So when the time comes, I'd like you do something."

"I said, of course. Do you want me to say *kaddish*?"

"*Kaddish?* I don't know what you're talking about. Just do something that says I was a Jew."

When Frankfurter died in 1965, Lou Henkin said *kaddish* at a private memorial service in Washington, D.C. Among those present were Lyndon Johnson, who was then president, and former Secretary of State Dean Acheson. "I explained that it was not a prayer for the dead but a *magnificat,* a song of God's praise," Professor Henkin said.

Eight years later, in 1973, when Professor Henkin's father died, some of his students started a tradition at Columbia Law School, right in Professor Henkin's office. Every afternoon, Jewish students would gather there so that he would not have to seek out a *minyan.* He could say *kaddish* without leaving the Law School. When his year of mourning was finished, students kept coming. That daily *mincha minyan* continues to this day, almost thirty years later.

12

In January, our *tertulia* guest was Rabbi Steven Greenberg, a Yeshiva University-trained rabbi who was coming to terms with his homosexuality. I remembered
Rabbi Greenberg, who wore a black *yarmulke* and *tzitzit,*
from my years as a regular on the Manhattan Jewish dating circuit. I'd see him socializing after synagogue services
or out on a date at one of Manhattan's kosher restaurants.
Now, in his forties, he said he had to face the truth. He was
gay. He also had to face his Orthodox Jewish tradition,
which called homosexuality a *to'eva,* an abomination.
Rabbi Greenberg did what any good Jewish scholar would
do when faced with a problem: he went to the rabbinic
sources. What emerged from his investigation was his new
interpretation of the scripture and commentaries in light
of modern medicine and psychiatry. It was fascinating but
also, in a way, heartbreaking to watch him struggle to be
true to a system that ultimately could only reject him.
Our men's group, proud to be both Orthodox and open-
minded, listened sympathetically but was far from con-
vinced. But while some of his ideas seemed farfetched,
Rabbi Greenberg's integrity and struggle were impressive.

We had a dozen men that night, more than enough for
a *minyan,* so we concluded with *ma'ariv.* When we first

convened the group in 1998, we had no intention of making it a prayer group, but one of our members was saying *kaddish* for his mother. We instituted a *minyan*. Now that I was saying *kaddish* for my father, we revived the service.

Before we finished for the night, we always pulled out our calendars and Palm Pilots and set the time and place for the next *tertulia*. We'd also propose a guest or a topic. "Role models," I suggested after we all agreed on a date. "Let's talk about the role models in our lives." There was some grumbling, because I had been trying, unsuccessfully, to get a conversation about fathers going for some time, but everyone was eager to go home, so role models it was. At least I hadn't proposed talking about my father.

When we met in February, the group wasn't finished with homosexuality. With Rabbi Greenberg not in the room, the comments were much more biting. Who is he kidding? He's rewriting the tradition! You can't be both Orthodox and gay!

After an hour and a half of this, I piped up: What about role models? That's what's on our official agenda, I reminded the group. Let's go around the room. Everyone looked at his watch. We always finished at 11:00 P.M. and it was already 10:30. We could handle half an hour of this, they seemed to be saying.

One fellow, a doctor, talked about a great surgeon who influenced him. My friend Allan, the music critic, spoke about John Lennon. Jackie talked about his rabbi, who was also a law school dean. I spoke about Abe Rosenthal, who guided my career at the *Times,* and my cello teacher, Heinrich Joachim. My friend Fred, a Wall Street portfolio manager, mentioned a youth-group leader who influenced him, an economist he worked with, and a guitar player he admired. "I've had a lot of role models," he said, "but ultimately I realized that they were all flawed."

"I keep coming back to my dad," Fred added. His father, a Polish Holocaust survivor who came to America with nothing, built a successful business and raised a family. "He's not perfect, but he's a good, solid man."

That hit me hard. I never considered my father a role model. In some ways, he was my antimodel. He was in business; I wanted to make my living writing and teaching. He lived most of his life in Hartford, to my mind a small town; I was a New Yorker and proud of it. When I'd needle him about being too modest, he'd say: "I don't want to set the world on fire"; but I *wanted* to set the world on fire.

But wasn't I also like my father? My father had a passion for what he believed in but an open mind toward others. My father loved Judaism and had a deep emotional connection to the music of the synagogue. My father loved to study sacred texts. My father had a strong ethical sense that he stuck to even when it meant economic loss. My father loved Israel. My father hated competitive sports but loved to swim. My father built community everywhere he went.

Sure he wasn't perfect, but was I, as Fred suggested, concentrating too much on his flaws?

In the year I said *kaddish* for my father, I began to realize that he was more of a role model for me than I was ever able to acknowledge while he was living.

Spring

1

I was eager for the coming of spring but also anxious about what it would bring. Two important events were on my calendar, both of them in Israel: the trip of my Covering Religion class to the Middle East and the unveiling of the monument at my father's grave. The Jewish custom is to have a formal service at the cemetery soon after the memorial stone is set in place. The unveiling service, more intimate than the funeral, is held within a year of the death, but after the immediate shock has subsided. Close friends and relatives gather to recite psalms and share memories. *Kaddish* is said.

Teme thoughtfully timed the unveiling at my father's grave to coincide with my class trip to Israel. Dov had been in Israel for the *shiva*. Shalom came soon afterward and was there for the end of the *shloshim*. I would represent my father's sons at the unveiling.

I built in some extra days both before and after the class trip to visit family in Israel and attend the unveiling. I had been to Israel almost every year since my father had moved there in 1992. For me, visiting Israel meant visiting my father. But this trip was very different. I would, for the first time, come face to face with the tangible reality of his death. I didn't want to wait for the unveiling service for my first visit to his grave. Shalom, a Middle East studies professor at Emory University, was in Israel on a teaching fellowship so I asked him to join me at the cemetery soon after I arrived.

Har HaMenuchot is on a hill on the outskirts of Jerusalem. By regulation, the memorial stones there are all horizontal, poured-concrete slabs. Each one looks just like the next; the only thing that distinguishes one from another is the name, date, and perhaps a biblical verse of tribute. On past visits to Israel, I had accompanied my father to Har HaMenuchot to visit the graves of his parents, Sam and Nettie, who like my father lived most of their lives in Hartford and then moved to Israel late in life. When we'd go to the cemetery, my father would matter-of-factly point out an empty burial plot adjacent to my grandparents. "That is where I will be buried," he'd say. I'd jab him playfully in the ribs and say, "Cut it out, Dad." He'd repeat, "That's where I'll be buried." Then he'd add with a smile, "After one hundred and twenty years."

Although I had been to the cemetery many times, I wasn't sure I could locate the family plot. The cemetery is vast. I asked Teme for the coordinates. She told me to enter the cemetery from the main parking lot, take the road that goes down the hill, walk until I found the blue door on a small stone building, take the staircase on the left, and go up two flights, and I'd recognize the family plot. "When you get to the path, you'll first find your grandparents and then your dad."

Shalom and I wandered through the cemetery in the hot sun but couldn't find the family plot. There were just too many roads, paths, staircases, and blue doors and far too many poured-concrete monuments. We saw that, even in death, Jews gathered in neighborhoods. We walked through a series of plots where all the names were French, another where the names were German, and yet others where the names were Spanish and Russian. Shalom, ever the professor, was fascinated. "This is like a trip through Jewish history."

It was fascinating, but we never did find my father's grave that day. After an hour of looking, we gave up. I was disappointed but in a sense relieved. I could put off confronting the reality of my father's death just a little while longer.

2

That night I couldn't sleep. I kept looking at the digital clock next to my bed. I was acutely aware that while I was in my Jerusalem hotel room, my students were at Kennedy International Airport boarding an El Al jet for the ten-hour trip that would bring them to Israel the next morning. My mind was racing. What if something went wrong? What if there was a terrorist on board? What if the plane crashed? I kept thinking of the teenagers from a small town in Pennsylvania who died in 1996 when TWA flight 800 exploded moments after take-off from Kennedy Airport. There had been sixteen of them, all members of the French club of Montoursville High School, happily going off to realize a dream of visiting Paris. Despite all their careful plans, the high school group never got to France. The picture that ran in all the newspapers was a final group photo of the students before they left for the airport. I kept seeing their smiling and eager faces in my head.

Then I started envisioning the graves of my students. Sixteen slabs of poured concrete on Har HaMenuchot, one indistinguishable from the other. I dreamed that I was running through the cemetery looking for their graves. There were groups of graves from Russia, from France, from Spain, and from Montoursville, Pennsylvania. I woke up in a sweat. How could I ever explain this to their parents? Where did I ever get the idea to bring a class to the Middle East? It was all a mistake. Maybe it wasn't too late. Maybe I could still call New York and stop the plane.

When I woke the next morning, I immediately turned on the radio. No news of planes crashing in the night. Thank God.

I made my way to Ben-Gurion Airport near Tel Aviv and watched the skies as their plane arrived. I normally keep my students literally at arm's length. I am very careful not to show physical affection, but when they got off the plane and walked into the Ben-Gurion terminal that morning, I hugged each one.

From then on I stopped worrying. The spring of 2000, with the Israeli–Palestinian peace process in full swing, was a time of relative calm in Israel. The bus bombings and suicide bombings that had once—and would soon again—grip Israel were gone. There was calm in the Palestinian territories and on the borders that Israel shared with its Arab neighbors. Many Israelis took vacations in Egypt's Sinai desert and Jordan's ancient city of Petra.

Our study tour went beautifully. We had a bus and a guide and the wisdom and good humor of my Columbia adjunct, Rabbi Michael Paley. We danced with Sabbath worshipers at the Western Wall, walked alongside Christian pilgrims on the Via Dolorosa, and took off our shoes to enter the Al Aksa Mosque. We traveled north, visiting the Baha'i Temple, a Druze village, and Nes Amim, a Christian kibbutz. We spent a day writing reports from Nazareth on preparations for the visit of Pope John Paul II. And we stopped at several of the sites that the pope would visit a week later when he arrived in Israel. We joked that we were the pope's advance team, checking out the holy sites he would see.

In Israel, it was easy for me to continue saying *kaddish*. I would occasionally peel off from the group to catch a *minyan* in a synagogue, school, or hotel lobby. I had yet to see my father's grave, but I said *kaddish* for him each day.

A week into the tour, Adam arrived in Israel. He came to spend some time touring and to attend the unveiling. Adam arrived for the Jordanian leg of our study tour. We left Jerusalem on a Sunday morning, drove into Jordan via the Allenby Bridge, and headed straight for Amman. Sunday afternoon was spent touring around Amman and observing the preparations for the papal visit, which would start the next day. We met with Jordanian officials and Catholic prelates who were in town to greet the pope. Monday morning, we got up early to head for Jordan's Queen Alia International Airport, but first Adam and I put on our *tefillin* and prayed in our hotel room. There was no *minyan* (that I knew of) in Jordan, so I went that day without saying *kaddish*. Still, I couldn't help but feel that my father would have been pleased that his son and grandson were carrying on his tradition of prayer.

Of course, my father might have been shocked to know where we were going after our morning prayers. He was no fan of the pope. Like other Jews of his generation, my father laid at the Vatican's doorstep all the sins of the Catholic Church against the Jews, from the Inquisition to the Church's apathy during the Holocaust. He was suspicious of the pope's friendly overtures to Israel. We got to the airport and onto the tarmac in time to see the papal plane appear in the distance and land just a few feet from where we stood. Pope John Paul II emerged from the plane and greeted the assembled dignitaries, including Jordan's King Abdullah II. The Jordanian honor guard greeted the pope with considerable fanfare and the crowds lining the airport road shrieked their delight. They carried signs in English and in Arabic that said, "Welcome to the Holy Land, Holy Father."

Our group returned to Jerusalem that afternoon. The pope followed in short order. He visited the Western Wall and the Via Dolorosa and the Al Aksa Mosque. He met with the prime minister and the chief rabbi, and spent an emotional afternoon at Yad Vashem, Israel's Holocaust memorial museum. His message was of peace and reconciliation. The deep political and religious wounds that were so much a part of Israeli life—from the tensions between Israel's secular and religious Jews to the smoldering relationship with the Palestinians—seemed to be papered over for a few blissful days.

In the midst of all this papal excitement, my students left Israel for New York, but I stayed on with Adam for a few more days.

It seemed as though my father's entire *daf yomi* class came to the unveiling. These were his closest buddies in Israel, the men with whom he had learned Talmud every day for his last seven years. A number of my cousins, aunts, and uncles who live in Israel were there too. While I had dreaded encountering the grave, being in the company of these people whom he had loved made it easier. My father's gravestone, with his name etched in Hebrew, stood beside the graves of his parents just as he had foretold. In that, I found a measure of comfort.

With a *minyan* assembled at the grave, I faced the direction of the Western Wall and said *kaddish*. "My father loved three things," I told the two dozen people who gathered around his grave, "his family, the land of Israel, and Torah."

With regard to family, I first mentioned Teme and the nurturing relationship he had with her during their twenty-five year marriage. I spoke about how theirs was a model for me of a good marriage. And then I spoke about my brothers and me. "My father loved his sons, even if we did things a bit differently, even when we sometimes surprised him by pursuing our own paths. And my dad was proud of us, not only toward the end of his life, but throughout his whole life."

I then spoke about my father's love for Israel and how he had the courage, at the age of seventy, to start life all over again in the Holy Land. "I never saw him happier," I said. Finally I spoke about his love for Torah. "When people asked me what my father did in Israel, I'd simply say, *daf yomi.* Learning Talmud each day was the center of his life." I acknowledged the men he learned with—my father's *tertulia,* of sorts—and thanked them for sharing this passion with him.

"My dad is no longer with us, but the things he loved still live—his family, the land of Israel, and the Torah. I believe we can honor him and connect with him by being true to the things he loved."

When he was alive, Dad and I could go for weeks without speaking to each other. Now, in the shadow of his tombstone, I was looking for avenues to connect with him. What surprised me was how many there were. I realized that I had more in common with my father than I ever knew.

3

Later that day, Teme and I went through some of my father's personal effects. There were old photos and family mementos that she wanted me to have, items like my grandfather's birth certificate from 1886 and a photograph of my grandmother's class at the Hartford Talmud Torah in 1903 (there are fifty-one boys pictured and one girl, Nettie Finkelstein). My father saved newspaper clippings about his father's involvement in Hartford politics (Grandpa Sam served three terms as Hartford's Police Commissioner in the 1920s) and religious documents, such as the 1939 bill of sale for two seats at the Beth Hamedrash Hagodol Synagogue on Garden Street. Probably most representative of my family's history was a business card from Finkelstein's, the clothing store founded by my great-grandfather, Nettie's father, Ephraim Finkelstein. The little card told the family's story:

FINKELSTEIN'S, ESTABLISHED 1898.
OPEN EVENINGS UNTIL 9.
CLOSED FRIDAY NIGHTS AND SATURDAYS.
OPEN SATURDAY NIGHTS AFTER SUNSET.
SELLING CLOTHES TO THREE GENERATIONS.

My family was the ultimate modern Orthodox family, involved in the world and yet loyal to the dictates of our faith. For three generations and counting.

One picture in my father's papers took my breath away. It was an eight-by-ten color photo of Dad, looking ever so dapper in a white dinner jacket and bow tie, with his three sons, all in ties and jackets. His arms are spread wide, embracing me on his right and Shalom on his left. Dov stands in the center. The portrait was taken at Sam and Nettie's fiftieth wedding anniversary celebration in 1961, at the Statler Hilton Hotel in Hartford. All four of us are wearing gold-colored silk *yarmulkes* (for the "golden anniversary") and yellow carnations in our lapels. It is a family portrait that, despite our broad smiles, is somehow incomplete. A father with three sons, but no wife or mother in the picture.

I took the photograph, but I wanted more. I was hoping, naively to be sure, that among my father's papers would be the picture I craved—a shot of my mother and father together, real evidence of their union. But it was not to be found. Not here. Not in my mother's papers. Nowhere.

4

S oon after I returned to New York, I got word that my forty-six-year-old cousin Elise Goldman was terminally ill with cancer. Elise, who grew up in Hartford, lived in Florida with her husband, Murray, and their ten-year-old daughter, Shanna. Elise died in late March and the family assembled to bid her farewell a few days later in a cemetery in Woodbridge, New Jersey. I saw a lot of Elise when we were children, but had lost contact with her over the years. I had never met Shanna, but knew who she was right away when I saw her at the funeral. With big hopeful eyes, a ready smile, and a head of curly black hair, she looked just like her mother.

The family on my father's side is a large one; I am one of fourteen grandchildren of Sam and Nettie Goldman. My cousins and I had gathered before at other family funerals and memorial services, but this one was different. This funeral was for one of our own. Elise was the first of our generation to die.

But as we gathered in sorrow and in pain, we were surprised to find that it was Elise who was concerned about us. Before she died, she penned these words, which were read by our cousin Donna at the funeral: "I feel badly about the pain I have caused through my passing, and yet I could not have waited any longer. I know what awaits me and it is wonderful. In the twilight of death between this world and the next, I could get brief glimpses."

She wrote that she did not fear death and implored us not to grieve. "Remember me with joy and health, and rejoice with me that I am whole again and needn't suffer anymore." As we heard her words, it was almost as if she were standing beside us at her open grave. "When you bury me," Donna read, "do not imagine me below the earth, but above it, soaring to greater heights on the wings of those who have gone before and return to help me make my journey from the darkness to the light.

"May your pain be healed in God's light as he has healed mine. I love you all, now and forever."

Elise's brother, Ian, said the special *kaddish* that is recited at the grave, and then we all offered personal words of condolence to the members of the immediate family.

After a few minutes, someone suggested that we *daven mincha.* Ten men assembled, and Ian led the prayers. While it would have been inappropriate for me to join Ian in the special graveside *kaddish,* the *mincha kaddish* was supposed to be recited by all the male mourners present. Still, I felt odd about saying *kaddish* with Ian. How could one compare the two losses? I was saying *kaddish* for a seventy-seven-year-old grandfather who had died seven months earlier. Ian was saying *kaddish* for his forty-six-year-old sister, a young wife and mother, whose grave was still fresh.

Conscious of this, I said the *kaddish* quietly, in an undertone, so as not to draw attention to my loss. But afterward, an older cousin came over to me. "Who were you saying *kaddish* for?" he asked. I was taken aback by the question. "My father, of course." "You're still an *avel?*" he asked. "My father died seven months ago," I told him. "Oh," he responded, "I thought it was longer ago than that."

New graves make us forget the old.

5

Driving home from Elise's funeral, I had an awful thought.

My brothers and I were the first cousins on either side of our family to lose both parents, the first to be completely orphaned. My parents were not the oldest in their families. My dad, in fact, was the youngest. All of my mom's sisters were still alive, as was the widow of her deceased brother. In other words, all my cousins have at least one parent. My brothers and I have none. Why do I have this awful feeling that it has to do with divorce? My parents' lives were somehow flawed. They got divorced; they died before their time. It's a terrible thought, I know, but I can't help thinking it.

6

There are two ways that Orthodox Jews make Passover. One is to thoroughly clean the house, take out the Passover pots and pans, dishes, and flatware, shop like demons, and cook around the clock. The other way is lock up one's house and go to a kosher hotel for the eight-day holiday. The hotel route has become increasingly popular for many families, especially ones where both parents are working. For Passover during my year of *aveylut,* Shira and I took the kids to the Rye Town Hilton Hotel, a resort about an hour north of our Manhattan apartment. Shira's parents and her brother and his family also came to celebrate the holiday there. We enjoyed one big *seder* together, and no one had to cook, serve, or clean up. (No one in our family, anyway.)

Spending Passover at hotels was very familiar to me. For years, my father, my brothers, and I celebrated Passover at a resort called Weiss' Farm, a family-run inn in New Jersey. When my mother married Jack, he brought us along for Passovers to the more upscale Catskill resorts, such as Grossinger's and The Concord. Seders for the first two nights and Borscht Belt entertainment for the rest of the week.

All these hotels also had morning, afternoon, and evening religious services, so catching a *minyan* to say *kaddish* was easy. I divided my time between the dining room and the hotel synagogue.

The Rye Town Hilton was filled with people my parents' age, and many of them had known my mother and father. The Orthodox world is a small one. Not only did people know my parents, but they also knew that both of them had died. Men and women would come over to me and say things like "I went to school with your mother," or "I was friendly with your father." "I think of your mother often when I'm here," one woman said. "How she loved Pesach." "I visited with your father a couple of years ago in Israel," a man told me. "He was so happy." People would explain their connection. They belonged to the same synagogue, grew up in the same neighborhood, were related to relatives who were related to relatives who. . . .

Of course, I would also have these kinds of encounters when my parents were alive. A day or two later, when I'd talk to my mother or my father, I'd say, "I saw so-and-so and they said hello." Mom and Dad were always pleased to get these reports from the field. But now I was seeing people and collecting memories that I didn't know what to do with. How do you convey regards to those who are no longer among the living?

7

A few days after Passover is my mother's *yahrtzeit*, the anniversary of her death. If in life we are remembered on our birthdays, in death we are remembered on our *yahrtzeits.* Judaism has little interest in birthdays (the only ones that truly matter are the twelfth and thirteenth, the bat and bar mitzvah ages that mark the passage into adulthood). But the *yahrtzeit* has a long tradition that goes back to Talmudic times. Each year on the anniversary of a parent's death, the child must say *kaddish* in a *minyan* during at least one of the three daily prayer services. There are two somewhat contradictory customs regarding the observance of the *yahrtzeit:* to relive the enormous sadness of death and to celebrate the values and lessons of the departed. The first custom has led to the tradition of sadness, contemplation, and even fasting on the *yahrtzeit* of a parent. The second custom has led to the sponsoring of a celebration of the deceased that usually includes drinking a little schnapps in his or her memory. The latter tradition is much more widely observed than the former.

My mother's family would make a big deal of the *yahrtzeit* of her mother, Tillie Mehler, whom we all called Bubba, which is Yiddish for grandmother. For many years after Bubba's death in 1979, her children and grandchildren would gather on her *yahrtzeit* for a memorial at the home of my mother's sister Bracha. These began as solemn occasions with psalms read and words of Torah exchanged, but after a few years these gatherings turned respectfully raucous, with family members joking with each other and trading diet secrets (the family obsession) even as we feasted on Aunt Bracha's blintzes and cheesecake.

By the time my father died, I had observed three *yahrtzeits* for my mother. Each year, as I got further from the loss and my life got busy with other issues, the *yahrtzeit* for my mother got a little easier. With the passage of time, I was better able to focus on what my mother gave me in life rather than what was taken from me in her death.

In the year of saying *kaddish* for my father, however, my mother's *yahrtzeit* was a time of double-barreled sorrow. I re-lived not only her death but also my father's. The uneasiness that I felt back in October about saying *kaddish* for the both of them at *yizkor* on Sukkot had subsided. Now, saying *kaddish* for both of them came as a great comfort for the unspeakable double loss I had experienced.

From my mother's *yahrtzeit* and onward, there was a change in my *kaddish*. I was no longer saying it only for my father. It was the *kaddish* of an orphan, mourning for both his parents. I was, for the first time in a very long time, seeing them as a unit—my parents—and not only as my mother and my father. Did I need any greater reminder than this *kaddish*? My parents were dead.

On that day of my mother's *yahrtzeit*, I needed support. Adam didn't rush off for school, but joined me at the morning service at Ramath Orah. He also could be counted on to be part of the *minyan*, although by early spring the daily *minyan* was going strong.

I asked Rabbi Silverman if I could share a Torah thought after the service in my mother's memory. I reviewed some of the laws of Rosh Chodesh, the holiday that celebrates the beginning of each new month, for which my mother had a special affinity. She always made a particular effort to come to synagogue on the Saturday before Rosh Chodesh, when special prayers are said in the hopes that the upcoming month will be a good and blessed one.

Afterward, I invited everyone to make a toast, a *l'chaim*, in my mother's memory. Some people bring schnapps to the synagogue for such an occasion, but I thought that orange juice and some breakfast doughnuts were sufficient at that hour. Since this is an added meal, it is said that the *brachot*, or blessings, are said in the merit of the deceased.

Setting up a *l'chaim* was something my father would do. I remember how he would spend the last moments of the *daf yomi* class getting cake and schnapps ready for his buddies. Here I was performing a very Dad-like task for my mother. On this day, it felt right.

8

The president of our *shul*, Leo Chester, does not attend the morning *minyan*. He calls himself "not religious," but he is one of the most religious people I know. What Mr. Chester means is that he is not observant of many of the day-to-day laws of traditional Judaism. But no one I ever met better embodied the spirit of Judaism.

Mr. Chester, a survivor of the Nazi death camp at Auschwitz, does just about everything in the *shul*. He pays the bills, balances the books, greets new members, reloads the toilet tissue, sets the thermostat, licks stamps, and hands out candy to the children and synagogue honors to the adults. He oversees the part-time custodial staff and hires the young men who read the Torah each Shabbat. Mr. Chester makes sure there is food for the *kiddush*, the brief collation after the Shabbat services. He personally pours the schnapps. There is no job too big or too small for him. Many visitors assume that he is a paid employee of the synagogue. They complain to him if there was not enough cake at the *kiddush* or if the place was too cold. It's hard to remember that Mr. Chester is only a volunteer. His wife, Henrietta, good-naturedly teases him about his obsession with the *shul*. "We're going to move your bed in there," she jokes.

There are a few things that Mr. Chester will not do, however. He will not lead the services or read the Torah. He also will not speak publicly ("I'm not a speaker," he says). He makes only one exception to his no-speaking rule. Every year on Yom HaShoah, the day on the Jewish calendar set aside for Holocaust remembrance, he gets up and tells his story, the number the Nazis tattooed on his arm—133497—a form of witness to the hell he endured.

Mr. Chester, one of three children, was born in 1925 to a middle-class family in Cologne, Germany, a city with a Jewish population of 50,000. On November 5, 1938, just four days before Kristallnacht, he celebrated his bar mitzvah in the great Orthodox synagogue known as the Gluckengasser Shul. His was the last bar mitzvah in Cologne before the war. In the anti-Jewish rioting that then swept through Germany, his father's clothing store was smashed and looted and the family apartment was destroyed by fire.

His father, Joseph, hired smugglers to take the family across the border into Belgium. Under cover of night, they made their way to Antwerp, where they settled with cousins until they could find an apartment of their own. In 1940, the Germans occupied Belgium and the family fled to Liège, in the French part of the country, where they were told they'd be safer since the French hated the Nazis. In 1942, additional laws against the Jews were enacted in

Belgium. They could not work or own property, and they had to wear the yellow star.

Joseph Chester thought his status as a German soldier during World War I would protect his family, but one day in 1942, the Gestapo arrested his wife and their three children. They were put on a cattle transport—seventy-five to a car—to Malines, an old fort located between Antwerp and Brussels. Joseph Chester, who was not at home at the time, went into hiding in Liège, where he remained until the end of the war, not knowing the fate of his family.

When they eventually arrived at Auschwitz, Mr. Chester's mother and sixteen year-old sister were immediately sent to the gas chambers. Mr. Chester and his brother, Randolph, had numbers tattooed on their forearms and were put to work. Of the 1,800 on their transport, only 200 survived the journey and the "selection" that took place on their arrival.

The two brothers stayed alive by their wits. One day, as they were walking with other prisoners to their work detail, they spotted an accordion on the ground. Randolph, who had studied piano as a boy, said that he'd love to play an accordion someday when the war was over. A German officer overheard and said, "You know how to play?" Randolph, who figured he had nothing to lose, responded, "Of course."

The officer pulled Randolph out of the line and said,

"Come with me." He brought him to the officer's club, where the men were smoking and drinking. "Play," he was told. Randolph strapped on the instrument for the first time and managed a song and then another, and another. His ability to figure out the instrument saved him from the hard work outside. It also gave him an opportunity to pick up extra food and bring it back to the barracks to share with his brother.

In the winter of 1945, in the face of the approaching Red Army, the Nazis began to liquidate the death camps. At Auschwitz, approximately 56,000 men and women prisoners, the Chester brothers among them, were sent on what became known as the Death March. They marched for twenty days. People who stumbled or fell were shot by the Nazis. "The SS officers ran out of ammunition, so they began to hit people with the butts of their guns," Mr. Chester recalled. Those who survived eventually arrived at the concentration camp at Buchenwald, and from there they were sent to a mine in the Black Forest. The Chester brothers were liberated by the French in May 1945.

Mr. Chester, who was then twenty years old, weighed eighty-four pounds.

He and his brother returned to Belgium, where they were reunited with their father. They all came to New York in 1947. Mr. Chester got a job in Manhattan's Diamond District and eventually married. He and his wife moved to the Columbia University area and were living there in 1954 when Mrs. Chester's father died. Rabbi Serebrenick, then the spiritual leader of Ramath Orah, heard about the death from friends of the Chesters and decided to see if he could help. He came one Saturday after services and, in keeping with traditional Jewish law, did not use the elevator, but walked up eight flights to their apartment.

After the visit, Mr. Chester recalled, he told his wife, "If an older man like that can walk up eight flights to visit us, we must join his synagogue."

Mr. Chester served as the synagogue treasurer for more than thirty years. In the mid-1990s as the *shul* began to experience a revival and new, younger members began to assume leadership roles, Mr. Chester became the last of the older generation to play an active role on the synagogue board of trustees. He finally was persuaded to become synagogue president. He accepted less for himself, he said, than as a way to honor and represent the founders of the synagogue that only he among us knew.

Mr. Chester shuns all liturgical roles but one. At the point in the Sabbath service when the mourner's *kaddish* is said, Mr. Chester bellows *"kaddish!"* in a loud voice, and then joins the mourners in the prayer.

I know that older people often have many relatives for whom they say *kaddish*—parents, brothers, sisters, spouses, etc.—but Mr. Chester never takes a break. Every time there is a *kaddish* opportunity, Mr. Chester takes it. "Who are you saying *kaddish* for?" I asked him one day after many years of watching him.

"I say it for the six million who have nobody to say it for them," he said. "There were so many of them, I will never run out. I will never stop. For the rest of my life."

9

ince Mr. Chester does not like to speak in *shul* on a regular basis, it was usually left to me as one of the two synagogue vice presidents, to make the announcements right before the end of the services each Saturday. I had my routine. First I would welcome everyone—"visitors, members, and those who are not yet members"—to Ramath Orah. I'd thank by name the people who helped lead the services. I'd talk about coming events at the synagogue and in the general Jewish community. And then I'd give the times of the various prayer services for the rest of the Sabbath and the week to come, always making a special plea for help for the morning *minyan.* "There are people saying *kaddish*," I would say, without mentioning that I was talking about myself. "We could really use your help. Please join us at 8:00 A.M. on Sunday and at 7:00 the rest of the week." I'd finish by inviting everyone to the social hall for the *kiddush,* giving a preview if there was a special treat like *kugel,* cold cuts, or *cholent.*

On most Saturday mornings, I'd take my children with me to *shul* and give Shira the morning off. Judah is generally very independent but used to get rather clingy in a crowd. When I'd get up to make the announcements, he'd insist on coming up to the podium with me. I'd sit him down on the podium, his back to the congregation, and begin to speak. At first I was self-conscious about having him up there with me, but I found that people warmed to the idea. "Your son is so cute," a longtime member told me at the *kiddush* following the services. "I love seeing him up there with you. It reminds me of when we were young and our children were still here with us, although in the old days nobody would allow a baby on the *bimah*."

I soon got more comfortable with the idea and adjusted my routine. "On behalf of Judah and myself, I'd like to welcome everyone to Congregation Ramath Orah. Judah, can you tell everyone what time the *mincha* service will be today?" Then I'd whisper, "Tell everyone how old you are." "Four," Judah would shout, unaware that he was replying simultaneously to both requests.

When I'd finished the announcements and we'd left the podium, Judah and I would sit in the oversized red velvet chairs at the front of the synagogue and join in the concluding prayers. Judah would draw his name in the thick velvet with his fingers. When it came time to say the final *kaddish* of the service, I would gather Judah in my arms and rock back and forth, hugging him and thinking of my own father.

10

After the *minyan* on the morning of my mother's *yahrtzeit*, I picked up the *Times* and saw that Cardinal John O'Connor, the fiery archbishop of New York, had died the night before of cancer. I knew O'Connor well and read the obituary with great interest. I had covered him at the *Times* from 1983, the year he was appointed archbishop, until I left the paper ten years later. How odd, I thought, that O'Connor should die on my mother's *yahrtzeit*. It wasn't the first time their lives had intersected.

My mother fought cancer for more than a decade. But in early 1995, after a devastating recurrence, the doctors said that nothing more could be done to save her. "She is in the hands of God," they told us. The only hospice we could find that met our needs was a Catholic facility in the Bronx called Calvary Hospital, which was run by the Archdiocese of New York. On the day we brought my mother to the hospital, we were met by the medical director, Dr. Michael Brescia. He personally reviewed my mother's case and sat with us to explain the hospital's goals and procedures. The goal was palliative, he told us, explaining that everything would be done to make my mother comfortable and pain-free. No more operations, no more chemotherapy. Dr. Brescia was patient and kind.

He made us all feel that in this time of crisis he was concerned about all of us.

Calvary is a Catholic hospital and every room has a crucifix. With Dr. Brescia's blessing, we removed the cross and hung a *mezuzah* on the door. We did everything to make her room a familiar environment.

After getting my mother settled in her new surroundings, we thanked Dr. Brescia for his extraordinary kindness. "I don't know how you do it," I said. "You run a 200-bed hospice, but you make every family feel as if they're the only ones here."

"Well," Dr. Brescia responded, "it's not every day that the cardinal calls."

There are seventeen Catholic hospitals in the archdiocese with over 2,000 beds. To this day, I do not know how O'Connor knew that the mother of his former nemesis at the *Times* (I admired him and we had cordial relations, but I was, after all, a newspaper reporter and we did clash on occasion) was now a patient at one of his hospitals. Several days later, I wrote to O'Connor thanking him for his kindness. He responded that he was thinking of me in this difficult time and that my mother was in his prayers.

The *New York Times* obituary portrayed O'Connor as a fierce defender of Catholic tradition, who was not afraid to take on politicians and bureaucrats. He also was said to have had real gifts as a pastor who reached out to those in need. I had seen both sides firsthand.

11

There was always a great influx of people to Morningside Heights in mid-May. The Columbia campus would get a new coat of paint. Cracked sidewalks were plastered, new trees planted, and the flower beds refreshed. People wearing rented caps and gowns began to appear on the street and proud parents were everywhere. The graduation season was under way. Ten thousand degrees were awarded before an audience three times that number.

Our *shul* also got a little boost from the season. Students would bring their parents to see where they pray, and so for that month we had no trouble assembling the morning *minyan*. One morning I entered the synagogue and saw an old college classmate, Daniel Kurtzer, who was then the United States ambassador to Egypt. He was one of those friends whom I didn't see often but felt an immediate closeness to whenever I did. We had been editors of Yeshiva University's campus newspaper together. He went into diplomacy; I went into journalism. In May 2000, he was in New York to see his son, Yehudah, graduate from Columbia College.

Danny and I greeted each other warmly and then got about the business of praying. When it came time to say *kaddish,* we both stood. I was surprised to hear him say the prayer with me.

"For whom?" I asked somewhat delicately when we had finished.

"My father," he said sadly. "First night of Chanukah."

"I lost my father too," I said. "*Erev* Sukkot."

We both nodded. Words of condolence seemed superfluous. Each of us knew what the other was feeling inside.

It's tough being fifty.

12

The day after the Columbia graduation, I flew to Chicago for a meeting of the trustees of the Covenant Foundation, a board I sit on that gives grants in the area of Jewish education. Serving on this board afforded me the rare opportunity of being a philanthropist without spending my own money. The foundation was supported by the Crown family of Chicago, which controls General Dynamics, the huge defense contractor, and owns part of the New York Yankees, the Chicago Bulls, and Rockefeller Center. The Covenant Foundation, which gives away tens of thousands of dollars a year to Jewish causes, is one of the family's smaller philanthropic arms. Each year, the staff of the foundation goes through several hundred grant applications from schools, synagogues, and Jewish community centers and makes recommendations to the board. The trustees meet only twice a year, each December in New York and each May in Chicago. At the May meeting we choose the three recipients of the Covenant Award, the Jewish equivalent of the MacArthur "genius award," this one given to outstanding Jewish educators.

I told Dov that I had an early flight that Thursday morning and that he should be sure to cover the morning *minyan;* I wouldn't be saying *kaddish.* The weather in New York was clear, but at the airport I learned that there were delays in Chicago because of severe thunderstorms. At one point, I thought of turning around and heading back home, but then a flight opened up. We sat on the runway for an hour, and eventually took off. I arrived at the meeting an hour late. The board finished its business early that afternoon and, under darkening skies, I headed for the airport. O'Hare was in a state of frenzy. My 3:00 P.M. flight on American Airlines was canceled. I ran over to the US Air terminal. Nothing moving. By the time I realized that I would not get a flight out that night, all the airport hotels were booked. I took a cab back to the center of the city in a heavy downpour. I found a room at the art deco Allegro Hotel and then got on the phone with the airlines. I was confirmed on a 1:00 P.M. flight Friday afternoon. Shabbat did not arrive until 7:56 that evening, so I was sure I'd get home on time.

I got to the airport first thing Friday morning, hoping to get on an earlier flight. After a few hours, with the rain falling relentlessly, it became clear there would be no 1:00 P.M. flight. I called my travel agent and told her that she *had* to get me out of Chicago. She said she could get me a seat that night on the 9:55 flight. "You know that won't work," I cried. "I am a Sabbath observer." There was nothing she could do. I was spending Shabbat in Chicago.

Whom do I know in Chicago? Nobody. At first, I thought I'd just go back downtown and check into the Allegro. I'd find some kosher provisions in the supermarket and then hole up in my room until Shabbat (and the storm) had passed. Maybe I'd walk to the library or a museum. But then I remembered that I needed to say *kaddish*. I had already missed two days of *kaddish* because of this trip; I didn't want to miss saying *kaddish* on Shabbat as well. I called the local Chabad House, a community center run by the Lubavitch Hasidim, a group famous not only for their outreach efforts but also for their hospitality to Jewish travelers. The rabbi there told me that there were no synagogues left in downtown Chicago but that he could match me up with an Orthodox family in the suburb of Lincolnwood. "There's a nice Orthodox *shul* there," he told me.

I got myself a room at the Radisson Hotel in Lincolnwood and made arrangements to eat at the home of Fay and Reuven Weiss. It all worked out fine. The Weisses and their children were lovely, and they served great Shabbat food. Like Ramath Orah, the Lincolnwood synagogue was modern Orthodox and adept at welcoming visitors. In fact, when I walked in, I rubbed my eyes in disbelief when I saw a fellow Ramath Orah member, Tibor Herdon. Herdon, a salesman, had also gotten stuck in Chicago for the weekend; he was staying with the congregation's rabbi.

Still, I missed my family and couldn't wait for Shabbat to be over so I could get a flight home. But I did not miss a *kaddish* that Shabbat. I knew that my father would have been proud of me. After all, he told me that he was proud of the way I traveled.

13

Dear Grandpa,

Hi. It's me Emma. I miss you so much!!! In school we are writing letters and I decided to write one to you. Ya' know . . . it doesn't seem like you are dead. Since you live in Israel, I don't see ya' too much. It just seems like you haven't called. The year I lived in Israel we talked to each other a lot, but I never talked to you about your bar mitzvah. I need to know a few facts, like:

1. Did you read your whole Torah portion? I'm not. I'm doing only three aliyot. 2. Were both of your grandparents there??? Too bad mine won't be!! 3. Did you have a ton of fun?? I hope I will!!

I have to go, OK?
Love,
Your one & only granddaughter,
Emma

Emma wrote that letter—decorated with hearts and stars—in June, a few days before her bat mitzvah, which was held in two installments, one part in

June and the other in July. Since we pray in an Orthodox synagogue, Emma's bat mitzvah options there were limited. While bat mitzvah girls can give speeches in Ramath Orah, they cannot lead the main service or be called to the Torah. (They can participate in a special all-women's service, but that's it.) Shira, Emma, and I decided to have the religious part of Emma's bat mitzvah in July at Camp Ramah in New England, the Conservative Jewish camp that Emma attended. The camp practiced a traditional but egalitarian Judaism. In the presence of both male and female friends, Emma could be called to the Torah and read her bat mitzvah portion.

At Ramath Orah, however, her coming of age meant that she could no longer sit with me on the men's side of the synagogue. Ever since we moved to Manhattan when Emma was six, she had worked both sides of the *mechitza*. Now she had to find her place on the women's side. It was wrenching for both of us. In her pre-teen years she would pray alongside me for a good chunk of the service, just as her older brother had done in the years before his bar mitzvah. Now she was twelve, and I didn't want her to go. She was angry that she had to.

Concerned about what both Emma and I were going through, I went to talk with Rabbi Saul Berman, a professor at Yeshiva University's Stern College for Women, who has for some time been the unofficial spiritual advisor at

Ramath Orah. Rabbi Berman is one of modern Orthodoxy's visionaries. He has developed a philosophy of social engagement that goes far beyond the ritual obligations of the Orthodox. He is among the most progressive Orthodox rabbis when it comes to women's participation in Jewish prayer and ritual, encouraging women-only services and other innovations. But the *mechitza* is where he drew the line.

"It's part of growing up," he told me. "Emma has to achieve independence and find herself."

Rabbi Berman, who sat near me in *shul,* noted that Adam had also gained independence in the synagogue by dressing in his own style (Adam favored all black) and coming on his own (usually late). Now it was time for Emma to find her own place. "Yes," I said, "but Adam's transformation was organic—he developed at his own pace. Emma's transformation is being imposed on her."

Rabbi Berman and I discussed various innovations that could be added to the Orthodox service (short of taking down the *mechitza*) that could make women feel more part of the action. We discussed lowering the *mechitza* at certain spots so women could have better sight lines and allowing women to read certain prayers aloud, like the Prayer for the Government. We agreed to raise these issues with Rabbi Friedman.

In the meantime, I changed my seat so as to be near the

mechitza. In that way Emma and I could still sit together, although there would be a cloth wall separating us. It was not much of a solution. Emma lost interest and started spending less and less time in the sanctuary (although she still came to hang out with her friends in the social hall). To be truthful, I also missed sitting near my friends. After a few weeks I moved back to my old seat. Many of the "innovations" that Rabbi Berman and I talked about were soon forgotten.

14

Early on, Emma and Shira ruled out Ramath Orah as a place for Emma's June bat mitzvah party. And as much as I loved it, I had to admit the place was rather shabby. We looked around a bit for the right catering hall and soon settled on the spanking-new Columbia Hillel, the Jewish social and religious center on campus. The building, with walls of exposed Jerusalem stone and arched entranceways, had just opened its doors. Emma's bat mitzvah party was the first family celebration held there.

Some 200 family members and friends came to celebrate the occasion from the many communities we feel close to: Ramath Orah, Anche Chesed, Columbia, the *New York Times*, our apartment building, and the Bruderhof, a pacifist Christian community in upstate New York. But most of all, it was a kids' party. While the adults ate salmon, the kids feasted on kosher lo mein and pizza (Emma's favorites). While the adults tried to talk above the DJ's blaring music, the more than sixty kids present danced wildly to Jewish tunes. It certainly was lively.

Technically, I should not have been there. According to Jewish law, in the year of mourning for a parent, one should not attend a party, especially one with music and dancing. Back in December I had succumbed to the lure of music when I went with my friend Liz to hear the gospel rendition of the *Messiah*. And I had even gone to a party or two. I, of course, knew that I would fully celebrate Emma's bat mitzvah. I knew of observant friends who absented themselves from family weddings and bar mitzvahs when the band started to play, or who simply sat out the dancing. But I didn't want to diminish Emma's joy. I stayed, I danced, but I was fully aware that I was an orphan. Neither my mother nor my father was there to dance with me or with Emma. I didn't feel any guilt. I knew, in fact, that my parents would want me to keep dancing. But there was a certain heaviness in my step and in my heart.

15

In late June we hit another dry period at Ramath Orah's daily *minyan*. We went for three days without one. One day we were seven men and then for two days we got up to nine, but we never broke into the double digits. The diehards, however, kept coming. But on Thursday even I had to stay home, because Shira had to leave on an early flight to Washington for business. I had to get the children ready and onto the school bus. At 7:30, while I was serving breakfast, the phone rang. It was my friend Allan. "Professor Henkin insisted I call," he began. "We've got nine here. Can you make it?" I told him that I didn't have child care. "I'm sorry," I said. I felt awful. There was no *minyan* that day because of me. And no *kaddish*.

When we were in our second week of no daily *minyan*, one of my friends said, "Ari, you have to start thinking of yourself and not just the *shul*. Why don't you go somewhere else?" I explained that my goal was to get to *shul* to *try* to say *kaddish* and not necessarily to say *kaddish*. If I gave up, and went elsewhere, there'd certainly be no *minyan*.

But a few days later I did give up. I sent an e-mail to the synagogue board. "Today, for the third day in a row, there was no *minyan*. I think we have to think seriously about shutting down the *minyan* for the summer. Just so you know what's coming: I'm gone as of Monday, Allan is going on a two-week honeymoon, Dan is moving to the beach, Professor Henkin is going to Geneva, and on and on. We need to make a decision immediately."

I thought I knew the *shul* well, but the reaction from Mr. Chester surprised me. He was furious. "Never!" he responded. "You can't have a *shul* without a daily *minyan*. What am I to tell people when they call? Synagogue is closed for the summer? Nonsense." Mr. Chester, normally a gentle soul, lectured me angrily. "With or without you, with or without me, this synagogue will always be here. Ramath Orah will survive."

And so for the rest of the summer, Ramath Orah tried, at least, to have a daily *minyan*. Sometimes it succeeded, sometimes it didn't. But it opened every morning, like an old antiques shop that opened for business every day even if no customers came.

Summer

1

Manhattan, where we live and work, is no place to be in the summer. It's hot and crowded and confining at a time when kids, and maybe adults too, deserve to be outdoors, running free. Each summer since we moved to Manhattan, we've escaped to a bungalow colony in the foothills of the Catskill Mountains, an old-fashioned summer community called Rosmarin's. We chose it in large measure because of *kaddish*.

We began looking for a summer place in the winter of 1995, when my mother was in her final stages of life and I knew that soon I would be saying *kaddish* for her. As Shira and I combed the Catskills for an appropriate summer place, we knew we needed to be within walking distance of a *shul* so that I could say *kaddish* on Shabbat as well as during the week. We both had sweet memories of bungalow colonies from our own childhoods and wanted the same for our kids. But, to our disappointment, we found that the summer bungalow world of the 1950s and 1960s had changed drastically. It fell victim to two growing American trends: air-conditioning and two-parent working families. Family vacations now had to be squeezed into a week or two rather than spread over two months. And a luxury resort or a trip abroad sounded a lot more appealing than an unair-conditioned bungalow that had to be swept out several times a day. As a result, the summer resorts were dying off.

Two very different religious populations began to fill the abandoned Catskill hotels and bungalow colonies: rigorously Orthodox Jews and practitioners of Eastern religions. Catskill hotels became Hindu ashrams and Buddhist zendos. These were places where devotees (many of them, incidentally, born Jewish) could spend time in retreat with their guru while meditating and eating vegetarian food. The bungalows, on the other hand, are particularly suited to the ultra-Orthodox. The women in these communities who work outside the home tend to have jobs that give them summers off, so they spend two months in the country with their children, with the fathers showing up for weekends. The bungalow colonies also give these rigorously Orthodox Jews the security of being surrounded by their own. There are separate hours at the swimming pool for men and women and a dress code, rigorously enforced, that guarantees modesty.

None of these places suited our more progressive Orthodox lifestyle.

Driving back on the New York State Thruway after a disappointing expedition to the heart of the Catskills, we stopped in Monroe, New York. Shira had spotted an ad for Rosmarin's in the *Village Voice* and we decided to try this one last place. As soon as we got there, saw the cabins, and met the owners, we knew we had found our summer home.

Rosmarin's, a family-owned business since 1941, has eighty-five summer cabins on 110 acres on a ridge above Walton Lake. The colony and a nearby day camp are run by the third generation of Rosmarins. The family is Jewish, but their clientele is mixed. Jews predominate, but there are also Italian and Irish Catholics, and other non-Jews. Just about everyone is from New York City, mostly from Brooklyn, Queens, and the Bronx. Rosmarin's is a friendly and unpretentious place, and also one where we knew we could be ourselves without having to live up to anyone else's expectations of our religious observance. And it is less than a mile from a small Orthodox synagogue on the grounds of a Jewish summer camp, Camp Monroe. It would be an easy walk on Shabbat. During the week, when it's okay to drive to *shul,* there were other *minyanim* I could attend: one in a nearby Hasidic village known as Kiryas Joel and another in an Orthodox summer colony called Quaker Hill.

With these *kaddish* options assured, we signed up for Rosmarin's, which more than met our expectations. And when my mother died that summer, I sadly availed myself of all three of them. But with time, and particularly during the summer that I spent saying *kaddish* for my father, they all proved problematic. I never felt at home at any of them. They reminded me that while I call myself Orthodox, Orthodoxy as a whole has moved relentlessly to the right. My *shul*, Ramath Orah, is an anomaly, stuck in time—the 1950s perhaps—when Orthodoxy was more open and tolerant. Much of contemporary Orthodoxy, I discovered, was no longer willing to engage the modern, secular world. I always prided myself on being able to live in both worlds—the Orthodox and the secular. The Orthodoxy I discovered in Monroe clearly said that this was no longer possible, that one had to choose one or the other.

It was a rude awakening.

2

Only a handful of campers attended services at Camp Monroe. Although it is owned and operated by Orthodox Jews, it caters to a largely secular Jewish clientele. The worshipers, rarely more than twenty, are camp administrators and some local Orthodox people who live in Monroe year-round. When I started to pray there on Shabbat mornings, the welcome was rather icy. I didn't know any of these people, and I was confused by the reception I was getting.

I came every Saturday morning—walking a mile each way, rain or shine—but the regulars barely greeted me. No one asked whom I was saying *kaddish* for. No one would really talk to me beyond a curt *"Gut Shabbos."* I thought at first that they were just suspicious of a stranger, but soon I realized that they knew exactly who I was. The Orthodox world is a small one.

Something was obviously going on, and I wanted to know what it was. After weeks of cold shoulders, I asked if I could talk to one of the officials of the congregation. People kept putting me off until I was referred to the president of the synagogue, a retired high school teacher. I brought along a copy of my first book, *The Search for God at Harvard,* to give him as a gift.

"Every Jew is welcome in the *shul*," he began, but then he went on to lash out at everything he felt I stood for, including Yeshiva University, labeling as "a lie" Yeshiva's philosophy of synthesizing Torah and secular knowledge. "I see Y.U. as a tremendous danger," he said. But he saved his true fury for the *New York Times*. Not only was the paper "anti-Semitic," he said, but I was part of the problem. He hated the articles I wrote about Jewish religious issues. "Sometimes I wanted to rip them up," he said. "Sometimes I did." He paused for a moment. "But you're a Jew," he added. "A Jew in his heart is a Jew, so you are welcome."

I should have given up right then and there, but I still wanted validation. What did I write that was so offensive? I asked. "Your ideas don't come from a Torah background," he responded. "Your ideas come from your own thoughts, which is an ego-type thing." I told him that I'd brought something that might help him understand my approach, if not my sincerity. I handed him a copy of my book, but he refused to take it from me. "I don't know if I could read it," he said, pushing it away in disgust.

After that, I kept to myself. I didn't need to break into this crowd. I didn't need its approval. But I did need to say *kaddish*. I went every Shabbat that summer but did not return there in subsequent years. This wasn't Orthodox Judaism as I understood it. And it wasn't my father's Orthodox Judaism, either.

3

I found much greater tolerance and a warm welcome at Quaker Hill, the ultra-Orthodox summer community about two miles from Rosmarin's. The first time I visited Quaker Hill to say *kaddish* was on a Monday afternoon in late June, right after we moved into Rosmarin's. I made my way to the synagogue, which was at the center of the sixty homes that make up the community, and found a group of teen-age *yeshiva* boys waiting for the *mincha* service to start. I was hot and thirsty, and I asked one of the boys if there was a soda machine nearby. He said, no, there wasn't one in the colony but that I should sit tight and he'd be right back. He returned three minutes later with an ice-cold Diet Coke. I don't normally drink diet soda, but I was so impressed that this kid ran home to get me one that I opened the can and drank it down. I also had a mighty thirst.

Over the two summers that I said *kaddish* there, I met several people I knew from my childhood. Some people recognized my name from the *Times,* but regardless of how they may have felt about my reporting, they were friendly and welcoming. One man in particular stood out. He was tall, bearded, about my age, and wore his black hat at enough of an angle to show that he was different from

the rest of the crowd of black-hatted men. He prayed with
an intensity that I had never before witnessed. Hebrew
prayer can get very monotonous; it is virtually the same
every day. But this man, it seemed, concentrated on each
word he uttered, knitting his brow and pumping his hands
and head for emphasis. I moved my seat close to him just
to observe. His eyes were closed and he was oblivious to
all. As I listened to his words I realized that he was several
pages behind the rest of the congregation. He was in his
own world.

When he finished praying (long after everyone else had
left the synagogue), I introduced myself and he invited me
to his bungalow for tea. His name was Mordecai Kurtz and
he was an architect. To my surprise, I found out that he
was a graduate of my alma mater, Yeshiva University, but
that he felt drawn to the more rigorous ultra-Orthodox
world. He spoke reverently of his teacher at Yeshiva, the
great Rabbi Joseph B. Soloveitchik. Rabbi Soloveitchik,
known simply at Yeshiva as "the Rov," was his mentor in
prayer.

"In my freshman year, they said that the Rov was going
to have his own *minyan* for Ta'anit Esther," one of the
minor fasts on the Jewish calendar. "The Rov *davened* very
slowly, very deliberately. He put the *tallis* way over his
head and his *tefillin,* and said *slichos* [special penitential
prayers] with such *b'cheyos* [weeping], I was awed. The

davening took two and a quarter hours. I was hooked. I told myself: This is a man I am going to be close to."

During the course of his years studying and following Rabbi Soloveitchik, Kurtz developed his slow, methodical way of praying. A few years after graduating from Yeshiva University, he lost his father, a Polish Jewish refugee named Shimon. I asked him if he remembered the experience of saying *kaddish* for his father. "It seems like yesterday, literally," he said. Kurtz recalled going to *shul* each morning to say *kaddish* and, as a mourner, often having the honor of leading the daily service. One day, he said, several people in the congregation lost patience with him. "I was *davening* more slowly than the congregation was accustomed to *davening*," he recalled. "And one morning, it was a Monday, I was criticized publicly for taking too long. And the rabbi heard it but did not leap to my defense. I felt so low and abandoned. I got into the car and drove home and parked in front of my apartment building and for forty-five minutes I cried my heart out. How abandoned, how alone, how isolated I felt. I needed that catharsis and I was denied it and I was lost. For me, that was the quintessential experience of mourning."

4

I f for Mordecai Kurtz saying *kaddish* was a catharsis, for Rabbi Eli Shlomo Cohen it was, above all else, an obligation. Rabbi Cohen was the principal of the girls' school at Kiryas Joel, a village consisting of approximately 15,000 Satmar Hasidim that was located right outside Monroe. I would often go there to say *kaddish* during the week. Rabbi Cohen's father, Simcha Bunim Cohen, was a Hungarian-born Holocaust survivor whose wife and four children were killed by the Nazis. After the war, he settled among the Hasidim of Williamsburg, found work as a baker, remarried, and raised a second family. "My father died five years ago," Rabbi Cohen told me. "And that whole first year I never missed a *kaddish* for him. It was not easy. I am responsible for a school with twenty-three hundred girls. I had to build my whole day around *kaddish.*

"With every *kaddish* you say for your father, you don't know what you can do," he said with a sense of wonder and mystery. "It is a 'true world' over there. In that world you can't do any more *mitzvos* [good deeds]. The only way to get higher and higher—there are a lot of steps in *gan eden* [paradise]—is for your child to say *kaddish*. A child has to honor his father in life and in death. This is how you show honor."

Rabbi Cohen told me a story about the head of the Belzer Hasidic dynasty. "Yissocher Ber lost his mother. He knew that he wasn't allowed to go to weddings, but he had one that he wanted to go to. He took out his Talmud and began to explore whether there were loopholes in the law that would allow him to go.

"Yissocher Ber fell asleep. His mother came to him in a dream. 'If you would know the kind of pain you would cause, you would never go,' she told him. He woke up, put away his Talmud and stayed home. Didn't go to the wedding."

Rabbi Cohen added, "If you follow the rules, it is a big thing for the soul."

The story was chilling. But Rabbi Cohen's view of *kaddish*—indeed, the traditional view of *kaddish*—was not my own. To me, *kaddish* is more for the living than for the dead. I believe that in my daily recitation of the prayer, I was coming to terms with who my father was and who I am. If I missed a day of *kaddish,* I suffered, not my father.

When I die, I want my children to say *kaddish* for me, but for themselves, too.

Rabbi Cohen and I talked as he drove me around Kiryas Joel. As we approached one housing development, we saw a large group of toddlers playing in front of a building a few blocks away. "My *enicklech!*" he exclaimed, using the Yiddish word for grandchildren. He took out his cell phone and called his daughter. By the time we pulled up to the building, she had assembled her brood to meet us. "Zaidy!" the children exclaimed. Rabbi Cohen beamed. He introduced me to his daughter, who looked away shyly. I knew not to extend my hand. And he introduced all the grandchildren. "This is Simcha Bunim," he said, proudly pointing to one little boy, "named for my father."

I was touched by what I saw in the right-wing Orthodox worlds of Quaker Hill and Kiryas Joel. There was a fervor and a sense of generosity there that is often lacking in the rest of contemporary Jewry. These were places where I know people would reply with a heartfelt "amen" to my *kaddish*, but ultimately they were not my world, or the world of my father. Ever since my Sabbath-observant great-grandfather opened a store in downtown Hartford in 1898, we have been a family destined to struggle with the outside world and not cocoon ourselves in isolated communities.

5

I spent almost the entire month of July at our bungalow. It was peaceful, and I got a lot of writing and
reading done, especially when the younger kids were
in the day camp. I would take breaks only to go to *shul* so I
could say *kaddish*. During the academic year, I spend a
good deal of time giving speeches at conferences and
before synagogue groups, but during the summer my
speaking schedule eases up. One of the few engagements I
had that summer was at a fund-raiser for Zichron Shlome,
a Jewish organization that provides support for families
stricken with cancer. The idea behind the organization
is that not only does the individual with cancer suffer, but
the whole family is thrown into crisis. Zichron Shlome
provides such services as food shopping, baby-sitting, and
cooking help. I was impressed with the group and its executive director, and I was happy to be of help. The fund-
raiser was held in the home of an Orthodox family in
Monsey. I gave one of my stock speeches, "Jews in the
News," about how the press covers Jewish issues and Israel.

Afterward, I was introduced to a Hasidic man who, it
turned out, was the father of "Shlome," the boy for whom
the organization was named. In considerable detail, he
told me about his son and his two-year-long battle with

leukemia—the treatments, the doctors, the travel, the strain on the entire family. Shlome was seventeen when he died. His final words to his father were: "*Tati,* don't just say psalms for me, do something to help others." I was moved by the story. I decided to tell him something I had told no one else there. "Both my parents suffered with cancer; my mother died from it," I began. "That is why I decided to come here today." But I could tell that the man was still thinking about his son, wiping away the tears that would never dry. There was, I realized, no comparison. Losing one's parents may be sad, but it is part of the natural order. Our parents die and we go on. Losing a child is devastating, against all logic and against life.

6

At the end of July, Shira and I left for a week in Paris. We arranged for a baby-sitter to watch Emma and Judah at Rosmarin's while we flew to France to meet Adam, who was just finishing a month-long French-language immersion program in Nice. I had not been to Paris for twenty-five years, and Shira had never been there. We spoke excitedly on the plane about all there was to do and see. "We must go to the opera," I told her, remembering my experiences there back in 1975. But then a little voice inside my head said, "You're still in mourning, you shouldn't go to the opera. Why did you suggest that?"

We got to Paris just a few hours before Adam arrived on the train from Nice. We then set about exploring the city and found, much to my relief, that the opera was closed, as it is every August. One less internal battle to wage with myself. I was also relieved to find a *shul* just one block from the apartment we were renting in the Thirteenth Arrondisement. It was on the ground floor of an apartment building at Sixty-one rue Vergniaud. There was no sign outside, just a building number. Synagogue members explained to me that most Jewish congregations in France are unmarked, out of fear of anti-Semitism. This congregation, founded in 1973 by Jews from Algeria, was known simply as the Synagogue of the Thirteenth Arrondisement.

It was a Sephardic congregation, with traditions that were different from the Ashkenazic, or European, ones I grew up with. Sephardic Jews come from Spain, North Africa, and much of the Middle and Near East. Instead of having one prayer leader, the Sephardic custom is to have different worshipers lead the various prayers, often from their seats. I sat entranced as the melodies bounced around me. There were thirteen men the first morning I was there, most of them, like me, saying *kaddish*. Afterward, I was greeted warmly. My French is very poor, and the men did not want to speak English, so we communicated in Hebrew. When they learned I was an Ashkenazic Jew from New York, they shared a joke about the Roman Catholic archbishop of Paris, Cardinal Jean-Marie Lustiger, who was born a Jew in Poland and later converted to Catholicism. "Why does Paris have a Sephardic chief rabbi?" they asked. "Because the archbishop is Ashkenazic!"

Sephardic Jews are in fact in the majority within the Jewish community of France, which numbers some 600,000. Praying with this small group of Jews in the Thirteenth Arrondisement gave me a sense of religious adventure as I fulfilled my *kaddish* obligation. One of the men I met, Norbert Abenaim, a Moroccan-born civil engineer, was saying *kaddish* for his mother, who died during Sukkot, just a few days after my father. Norbert told me that he found the discipline of *kaddish* harder now than when he had said it many years earlier for his father. "My father died in Morocco, and I felt so distanced I needed to say *kaddish* every day," he told me. "My mother was with me in Paris and ailing for so long. I did so much for her during her life that I don't feel compelled to do as much now that she's gone." Still, he came to *shul* regularly.

Rumi Gerard-David, a retired building contractor who was born in Algiers, told me that when he lost his father seven years earlier, he knew virtually no Hebrew. "My father died and I did not know how to say *kaddish*," Rumi said sadly. "A friend from Jerusalem came to visit me during *shiva* and said, 'Now is the time. You must learn Hebrew. I will be back in a year to test you.'" Rumi told me that he spent the year of mourning learning Hebrew in memory of his father. "*Kavod l'abah shelee* [To honor my father]," he said in flawless Hebrew, pointing to the heavens. All these years later, Rumi still comes regularly to the synagogue and, he added, plays tennis every afternoon. "Those are my passions," he said.

7

When I returned to New York in early August, I had only nine days of *kaddish* left. The mourning period is determined by the Hebrew calendar, a system governed by the moon rather than the sun. The Hebrew date of my father's death was the fourteenth of Tishrei, and so the eleven-month period during which I was obligated to say *kaddish* ended on the thirteenth of Av. (The Hebrew year in which I completed *kaddish*, 5760, was a leap year, meaning that it contained an extra month in the spring—Adar II—so my eleven-month period did not include Elul, the month that precedes Tishrei, which it otherwise would have.) The reason *kaddish* is said for only eleven and not twelve months has to do with Divine reward and punishment in the afterlife. I had heard the rabbinic explanation many times before, but it was not something I wanted to think about in the context of my mother and father. So I just followed the rules.

But, for those interested: According to Jewish tradition, after death one suffers the punishments of *gehinnom*, or hell, before going on to *gan eden*, or paradise. The more sins committed in life, the longer the punishment. (As Rabbi Cohen of Kiryas Joel told me, the dead can do nothing about this; only the *kaddish* of their children alleviates the punishment.) But *gehinnom* has a time limit. No soul suffers there for more than a year. To demonstrate the belief that one's parents are not among the totally wicked who would endure a full year in *gehinnom,* the *kaddish* period is reduced—for all mourners—to eleven months.

Of course, I had trouble imagining my parents in *gehinnom* at all. I hated this rabbinic reasoning. But, still, I found great significance and satisfaction in saying *kaddish,* both in the cathartic power of the prayer and in the act of fulfilling the religious obligation. I know it is what my parents expected of me. They said it for their parents; I say it for them. To hell with *gehinnom.*

8

I spent the last nine days in scrupulous observance of *kaddish*. While I had slackened off at some points during the year, I wanted to round out the eleven months the right way. My friends at Ramath Orah were happy to have me back after my summer vacation. I was often the tenth man. And when I was the seventh or eighth or ninth, I'd call my friends and beg them to come and help us fill out the *minyan*.

On the morning of August 7, a friend who, like me, hails from Hartford, approached me excitedly as I entered *shul*. "That boy from our home state did good," he said. Still catching up on my jetlag from the Paris trip, I had not listened to the news that morning so I didn't know what he was talking about. "Joe Lieberman," he said. "Gore just picked him to run as vice president."

The news was a lift not only for Connecticut natives but for Orthodox Jews the world over. For me, Senator Joseph Lieberman of Connecticut personifies the very best in Orthodoxy—someone who is observant of Jewish law but still very much at the center of what is going on in the secular world. Al Gore chose him knowing that Lieberman would not campaign on Shabbat. One joke going around was that Lieberman told his running mate that he was available "24/6." In a Gore-Lieberman administration, Lieberman said, he would not routinely work on Saturdays but in the case of a national emergency, when American lives were at stake, he would, of course, make himself available, just as one is obligated to violate the Sabbath to save a human life. Lieberman gave examples of how, during his twelve years in the Senate, he had on a handful of occasions walked to the Senate on Saturdays to cast a deciding vote.

The American people seemed ready for someone like Lieberman, a Jew in public life who was not afraid to talk about his faith. The fact that he was the first Jew on a major-party presidential ticket seemed, to the delight of the Jewish community, to be perceived by the American public as a positive development in our nation's history. American Jews felt an unprecedented level of acceptance by this country's non-Jewish majority.

Throughout the campaign, I often thought how sad it was that my parents, who had experienced firsthand the difficulties in being observant Jews in twentieth-century America, were not around to relish the moment. After all, just like the Liebermans, the Goldmans are modern Orthodox Jews from Connecticut.

9

Ramath Orah was my first stop on those August mornings. But if despite our best efforts there wasn't a *minyan* at Ramath Orah, I would head down to Vorhand's synagogue on West Ninety-first Street.

Vorhand's is not easily pegged. If you took all the Orthodox synagogues where I said *kaddish* throughout the year and put them in a blender—and a shrinking machine—you'd get Vorhand's. It's tiny, no more than twelve feet wide and fifty feet long, but there seems to be room for everyone. There are Hasidic Jews, Sephardic Jews, the newly religious, the nonreligious, Wall Street bankers, journalists, and people one step away from being homeless.

There are three morning services, on the hour, beginning at 7:00. And they always seem to be able to make a *minyan.* People from the first service hang around to make sure there are enough people for the next. Inevitably, some latecomers relieve them. This means that while some are praying, others are having coffee, studying sacred texts, or reading the *New York Post.* Vorhand's sometimes reminds me of an Off-Track Betting parlor.

The rabbi at the helm, Zev Zvi Vorhand, was no more than five feet tall, but was a powerful presence in the synagogue. Born into a rabbinical family in Prague in 1912, he eventually became the chief rabbi of Czechoslovakia, and as such was able to help hundreds of Jews escape the Holocaust. He came to New York in 1950 and founded his *shul,* formally known as Congregation Hechal Moshe, shortly thereafter.

Even when Rabbi Vorhand was well into his eighties, no one who walked into the *shul* escaped his notice. He would walk over and greet the newcomer, ask where he was from, and then immediately start playing Jewish geography. "Baltimore? Oh, do you know Rabbi Steinberg in Baltimore?" he would ask (even though Rabbi Steinberg had been dead for decades). By the time I got to know Rabbi Vorhand, it was clear that his memory was failing. Each time I showed up he would greet me, ask my name, and ask where I was from. I didn't mind. He had sparkling blue eyes and the softest hands—"baby hands," his son, Moshe, called them—and his welcome was genuine.

Although I was not a regular, once I reminded the rabbi that I was an *avel,* he let me lead the services. On the thirteenth day of the Hebrew month of Av, August 15, 2000, I completed the eleven-month *kaddish* period for my father by leading the service and saying a final *kaddish* at Rabbi Vorhand's *shul.* I had fulfilled the obligation—both to my father and myself.

10

Now that I was no longer saying *kaddish*, I entered into a new phase in my year of mourning. I was technically still an *avel*—that would continue for another month—but you'd no longer know that if you *davened* with me in *shul*. In this system, you get the twelfth month off. My next *kaddish* responsibility was several weeks away, on my father's *yahrtzeit*.

But habits are formed over eleven months. When I came to the synagogue, I would sometimes reflexively join in the *kaddish* prayer. I had to stop and remind myself that I was no longer a regular *kaddish*-sayer. The one easy habit to break was getting out of bed early in the morning. Although I resolved to continue going to the morning *minyan*—at least occasionally—the lure of a warm bed and the prospect of just a little more sleep were just too great, and for the most part I stopped going to *minyan* during the week.

But I had one other mourning-related task to complete. I ordered a brass plaque with my father's name and *yahrtzeit* date from the synagogue office. Mr. Chester put it on one of the memorial boards at the back of the synagogue, not far from the plaque I had bought several years earlier for my mother. Next to each plaque is a tiny lightbulb that is turned on each year at the *yahrtzeit* and on the holidays when *yizkor* is said: Yom Kippur, Shmini Atzeret, Passover, and Shavuot.

During services one Shabbat a few days later, an elderly woman who was a longtime member of Ramath Orah crossed over to the men's side of the congregation during services and stood staring at the memorial boards. I went over to see if I could help her. "Who are you looking for?" I asked gently. She pointed to a plaque. "He was my friend," she said. "Nice man. I know so many of them." And then she added sadly, "I wonder why I'm not up there too."

11

On the first anniversary of my father's death, I got to Ramath Orah early and put on the white prayer shawl with the silver mantle that was once his. It no longer felt alien or too big. Over the year of mourning I had grown into it. It was now my *tallit*.

I very much wanted to say *kaddish* at Ramath Orah that day, so I let some friends know that I needed a *minyan* and they came. We were eleven men, and I led the service. "*Yitgadal v'yitkadash shemey rabah*," I said. Glorified and sanctified be God's great name.

With that prayer—said perhaps 1,000 times over the course of the last year—I completed the year-long process of mourning for my father. That day in *shul*, I especially felt the presence of God and the presence of my father. I had fulfilled my responsibility as a son. I brought my father through the transition from life to death.

After the service, I walked to the brass memorial boards at the back of the *shul*, found the plaque for my father, closed my eyes, and gently ran my fingers over his name. I switched on the little adjoining light in his memory and walked out into the morning sunshine.

Epilogue

I t's been three years since I finished saying *kaddish* for my father, and the daily morning *minyan* at Ramath Orah struggles on, occasionally with me but more often without me. Other mourners have taken my place. The *shul* regulars are still there, including Professor Henkin of Columbia Law School and Alan Kozinn of the *Times.* Dr. Schmeidler still gets there early and opens up the building. Mr. Sandberg, the Polish immigrant who lives down the block, blacked out again in *shul* one recent morning, this time with a stroke. Once again, Hatzolah, the Jewish ambulance service, carried him out. A few weeks later, he was back, but clearly the stroke took its toll. He sits motionless through the service and stares straight ahead. He no longer rises to say the prayer for health for his ailing wife. Melvin, the freelance writer who came to say *kaddish* for his mother, pretty much disappeared when the year of *kaddish* for her ended, but I still see him in the neighborhood.

I picked up some habits during my year of *kaddish* that I keep to this day. If I see someone saying *kaddish* in *shul*, I approach him, introduce myself, and ask who he is saying *kaddish* for. This might seem rude or intrusive, but I have found that most people are actually eager to answer. One elderly man told me he was saying *kaddish* for his mother, who had died when he was three years old. His voice cracked as he said the prayer in memory of a woman he never really knew, and I realized that comforting mourners is an on-going process. We can ask. We can listen. We can say "amen."

I remember how powerful a witness it was when my friend Elie came in from California and got up early in the morning to, as he put it, "say amen to your *kaddish*." I now try to do that for friends who are in mourning—not only during *shiva* but six or seven months down the road, when they are alone with their loss. I meet them at their local synagogue just to say with a simple "amen" that I haven't forgotten them.

One of the new mourners whom I have approached at Ramath Orah is a woman in her forties named Amy Silver. While women showed up occasionally during my year of *kaddish,* there was no steady woman mourner. It was a men's club. Now Amy comes every morning to say *kaddish* for her mother, who died in Florida in the summer of 2002. While most Orthodox women do not say *kaddish,* preferring to leave it up to their brothers, husbands, or other male relatives, Amy took on the *kaddish* responsibility after her mother's death. She grew up in a Conservative synagogue, she told me, where women saying *kaddish* was commonplace. "My mother said it for her father," she recalled. Amy does not seem as concerned about the lack of gender equality in Orthodox synagogues as some of the modern Orthodox women I know. "One rabbi told me that when the Messiah comes, men and women will be equal," she says.

Ramath Orah takes Amy's participation very seriously. "The guys are very supportive," Amy said. Her Hebrew is a bit shaky and she doesn't like saying *kaddish* alone, so when she is the only mourner present, a man recites it with her. When she can't make it to a synagogue, she has a backup: a Ramath Orah friend, a rabbinical student named Bryan Bramley, says it for her, keeping Amy's mother in mind.

Although Amy can't be part of the morning *minyan,* she's voluntarily taken on another role: she hosts a daily breakfast of coffee and bagels at the conclusion of the services. "I do this as a tribute to my mother," she said. The breakfast makes Ramath Orah a cozier place, a place more likely to get a *minyan* on a cold winter morning than a place without breakfast.

The summer after I stopped saying *kaddish,* a minor miracle happened in the *shul.* A philanthropist named Sam Domb, the owner of several New York City hotels, decided to restore the *shul* interior to its original beauty. He had the five-story-high dome repainted, the carpets replaced, the floors polished, and the pews restored, all of which gave the *shul* a special gleam. It was an act of unconditional generosity. Mr. Chester says that the place hasn't looked this good in forty years.

Rabbi Vorhand, the rabbi of the little *shul* on Ninety-first Street, died two months after I last said *kaddish* for my father in his *shul*. His son, Moshe, took over. My friend Rabbi Koslowe, the Jewish chaplain at Sing Sing, also died. I wrote Rabbi Koslowe's obituary for the *Times*. (Obit writing is a franchise I've kept up since leaving the paper. It is a freelance job that suits me: it keeps my byline in the newspaper and keeps me in touch with a broader community of mourners.)

In a very real sense, every one of the people I got to know in my year of *kaddish* has stayed with me. Each experience shaped me, whether it was the synagogue at Camp Monroe, where I was a pariah; or at Quaker Hill, where a nice young man gave me a soda on a hot summer day, or at the Synagogue of the Thirteenth Arrondisement, where I was the Ashkenazic outsider. Each person and each experience helped mold my consciousness about life and death and prayer.

I think about Rabbi Cohen, the Satmar Hasid, who told me that the dead can do nothing for themselves; only we can help them. I think of Mr. Chester, who vows to say *kaddish* for the six million every day for the rest of his life.

I think of the cathartic *kaddish* of Mordecai Kurtz, the architect.

I said *kaddish* almost every day for nearly an entire year. For eleven months, I got up early in the morning, looked for a *minyan,* and dutifully called out the ancient formula for praising God. Why? What good did it do? Jewish tradition teaches that *kaddish* eases the pain of the dead. What kind of pain do they experience? I can only imagine that the pain is the agony of not knowing.

To me, the hardest thing about dying must be the not knowing the end of the story. My mother and father left this world while their grandchildren were small and their sons were still settling down into jobs and homes and relationships. By any rational understanding, my parents will never know what happened to us all. But how could they *not* know? How can someone be part of the story one day and in the dark the next? After all, the knowledge, creativity, and love of my parents were not physical things that we could feel. They were beyond the physical. Those things can't just disappear, can they?

In a sense, *kaddish* keeps these essentials alive. Maybe *kaddish* in itself is a kind of afterlife. The one thing my parents knew with reasonable certainty was that we, their sons, would be saying *kaddish* for them. They would be physically gone someday, but their *kaddish* would live on. I like to think of it as more than a prayer. I think of *kaddish* as a portal for the dead to connect to life. For those eleven months, I'd begin the day with *kaddish* and then move into all the other realms of my life: my teaching, my writing, my parenting. My parents are gone but yet here.

Ten months after I stopped saying *kaddish* for my father, I was awarded tenure at Columbia. When I first got the good news from my dean, I sat down at my desk and cried. I so wanted to share the news with my mother and my father. No one would have appreciated it more. Still, in that moment of longing, I feel I connected with them.

I think of all the things my parents have missed. Birthdays, *seders,* Thanksgivings, graduations, my Adam's inspired piano playing, my Emma's starring role in a local production of *Annie,* my Judah's Suzuki cello lessons. It seems unfair that my mother and father can't be here. But perhaps through my missing them, they are.

I never did get that e-mail from my father in heaven that I was hoping for in the weeks after his death. I've come to accept that he is in a place where e-mail is not necessary. My parents know how we're doing; and, in a real sense, we know how they are. I can only imagine heaven as a place where that which is broken has been repaired. My father's weak heart. My mother's cancer. There are no bills to pay, no traffic jams, no arguments, no fights, no deadlines, maybe even no divorce.

I often think of the comment Emma made during the

shiva for my father. "Do you think Grandma and Grandpa
are married again in heaven?" she asked.

A few weeks after I finished saying *kaddish,* I got a call
from my cousin Debbie Kram in Boston. She said she
was going through some family documents and came
across an undated wallet-size wedding photograph. "I
think it's your parents," she said. "Do you want me to send
it to you?"

I didn't open the letter for a few days after it arrived,
but let it sit on my desk. I had never seen a picture of
them together, let alone one on their wedding day. The
thought of it at first frightened me. One night, when everyone in my house was sleeping, I slit open the envelope and
there were my parents: young, happy, healthy, smiling,
beautiful—and together.

At that moment, I realized that with my parents gone
from this earth, they are liberated from time. I can
remember them at any point during the timeline of their
lives. I don't have to remember my mother slowly dying of
cancer at Calvary Hospital in the Bronx. I don't have to
remember my father the way I last saw him in Jerusalem,
as a frail and ill old man. I can pick the moment. I remember my mother lighting the Sabbath candles on Friday
night, the house full of the smell of her savory Sabbath
cooking. I remember my father singing gently under his
tallit in *shul.* I remember my mother all dressed up and

smelling like a bouquet of flowers, on her way out to a fancy dinner. I remember my father throwing a ball to me at his favorite beach on the Connecticut shore. I remember my mother driving her convertible, the top down and the air-conditioning at full tilt. I remember a lot of wonderful things. I can even remember my mother and father together. I carry that picture from their wedding in my wallet. It is a sweet memory of their lives that nothing— not even divorce and death—can take away from me.

ACKNOWLEDGMENTS

Many people had a hand in making this book a reality. I would like to thank my agent, Bob Markel, for being there when I needed him. I would especially like to thank my editor, Altie Karper, for never letting up. I didn't know it was possible to ask so many questions, all of them beginning, "How did you feel when . . . ?" A more devoted editor I have never known.

I am grateful to the many mourners who let me into their lives. I learned from every encounter.

I got valuable comments from friends and relatives who were kind enough to read all or parts of the manuscript, including my cousins Debbie Kram and Debra Kolitz, and my friends, Rabbi Etan Tokayer, Rabbi Joseph Telushkin, Dan Victor, Allan Kozinn, Jack Nelson, Blu Greenberg, Stephen Fried, Carolyn Hessel, Yehudah Cohn, and Rabbi Elie Spitz. My brothers, Shalom and Dov, also read the manuscript. Their perspective is different from mine, but I thank them for their love, support, good counsel, and tolerance.

I would also like to thank my colleagues at Columbia who supported me during the process of writing this book, especially my dean, David Klatell, and my friends Samuel G. Freedman, Michael Shapiro, Rhoda Lipton, Julie Triedman, Barbara Fasciani, Eryn Curfman, and Chenese Wilson.

I am especially indebted to my teachers in Torah, including Rabbi Norman Lamm of Yeshiva University, Rabbi Saul Berman of Edah, Rabbi Nathan Laufer of the Wexner Heritage Foundation, Rabbi Michael Paley of UJA-Federation, and Rabbi Steven Friedman of Ramath Orah. My thanks also to my friends Ruth Wheat, Bryan Bramly, Judith Clabes, Ross Winter, and Herschel Manischewitz, and to my in-laws, Henry and Rochelle Dicker, and my nephew, Daniel Goldman.

No one lived through the experience of this book with me more than my wife, Shira. She mourned with me for my mother and later for my father, and lovingly helped me craft this work. I dedicate the book to my children, Adam, Emma, and Judah. Throughout the process of mourning, my children constantly affirmed for me the simple joys of life. They allowed me to laugh through my tears. The stories in this book are mine, but the legacy is theirs.

ABOUT THE AUTHOR

Ari L. Goldman is the author of *The Search for God at Harvard* (a *New York Times* Notable Book) and *Being Jewish.* He was born in Hartford, Connecticut, and was educated at Yeshiva University, Columbia, and Harvard. From 1973 to 1993 he was a staff reporter for the *New York Times.* Mr. Goldman, currently a professor and assistant dean at Columbia's Graduate School of Journalism, is a regular contributor to the *New York Times* and the *Jerusalem Post,* and he lectures widely throughout the United States on both religion and journalism. He lives in New York City with his wife and three children.